HISTORY *of* PROSPECT VALLEY

Dedicated to the Memory of the Families
— of —

JOHN and PHOEBE (CONAWAY) CHALFANT

MELVILLE and CHRISTENA (CHALFANT) BARTLETT

— By —

NETTIE BARTLETT COOPER

July, 1940.

This volume was reproduced from
An 1940 edition located in the
Publisher's private library,
Greenville, South Carolina

All rights reserved. No part of this publication may be reproduced,
stored in a retrieval system, transmitted in any form, posted
on to the web in any form or by any means without the
prior written permission of the publisher.

Please direct all correspondence and orders to:

www.southernhistoricalpress.com
or
SOUTHERN HISTORICAL PRESS, Inc.
PO BOX 1267
375 West Broad Street
Greenville, SC   29601
southernhistoricalpress@gmail.com

Originally published: Richmond, VA 1940
Copyright 1940
By: Nettie B. Cooper
Reprinted by: Southern Historical Press, Inc.
Greenville, SC
ISBN #0-89308-951-6
All rights Reserved.
Printed in the United States of America

NETTIE BARTLETT COOPER

MELVILLE AND CHRISTENA (CHALFANT) BARTLETT

History and Family Genealogies

THE history of a community and family genealogies do not concern any except those who have at sometime lived there or who are a kin to those whose names are mentioned within. It is not expected to be of any interest whatsoever to others. Interest in family history or genealogy has increased much of late. There is, more than ever before, valid reasons for preserving authentic lineages.

Just traditional hearsay is not dependable for accuracy. There must be some legal records, such as are in county court house files, dates of births, deaths, marriages, wills, deeds, etc. Then old church records, newspaper files and family Bible records. Many of these have been forever lost through fires, floods, and even wars.

I have made a supreme effort to get these as nearly accurate as possible, however some of the dates seem to contradict each other; these errors may have been made in the many times they were re-written and copied.

It would be interesting indeed, if one could open the unwritten pages that would tell us what happenings took place in this beautiful valley in the remote past. This we do know, that long before the coming of the white man, the Indians were the occupants. It is impossible for us to know just who were the first palefaces to actually begin living here. We only know who obtained the first land grants that gave legal possession.

Some brave souls dared to come and blaze a trail for future generations, even though they built block houses and stockades, in which to fortify themselves from attacks by the Indians, many were killed and some carried away in captivity.

On another page in this book is a description of the location of one of these stockades, but not much information has been recorded as to how often they were obliged to use it. Up until a few years ago, the grave of an Indian could be seen in the Laurel Thicket, which is now covered by the water of the reservoir.

A great portion of this territory was still virgin forest with the exception of small clearings around the houses in the 1700's. The story of these pioneers would be the same as that of all those who dared to move farther westward into the great wilderness. Adventurous families in covered wagons, horse- and mule-packs carrying all their worldly goods, tools with which to build houses, and implements, and seed for raising crops; clothing, etc. Our forefathers had to be resourceful. Before they could begin to live, they had to cut trees to clear the land for crops and build homes. That meant hard toil, with limited equipment for pulling out stumps and rocks, before the land could be planted with seed. Besides, two or more would have to be watching with leveled guns to protect the workers from the lurking red men.

There was work for every one, since everything had to be home made; builders used wooden pegs for nails till in later years when "pig iron" was brought from east of the mountains, then nails and bars were forged to be used in making plows, furniture, looms, chests, etc. The women spun flax into thread and wove cloth for all purposes, later combined it with wool and made even the men's "linsey woolsey" suits. They also knit socks and stockings for the entire colony. Fires were lighted with flint and steel; lights were long hand dipped tallow candles. The cloth was sometimes very beautiful, the thread was first dyed with barks and herbs. If a caravan of pack horses succeeded in getting through alive with supplies from "back east," then there would be various luxuries, such as dye stuffs madder and analine for reds, logwood for black, and blue vitriol. Walnut hulls made a rich dark brown. Hickory bark made yellow. I have a quilt made of woolens spun in the Chalfant and Conaway families. The main part is a plaid flannel, the colors are still clear and rich, of brown, red, yellow, blue, and green. The green was first dyed yellow with hickory, then re-dyed with blue vitriol. I've heard my grandmother Chalfant say she had seen her mother (Mrs. Jeremiah Conaway) put skeins of white yarn and skeins of yellow yarn (hickory dyed) into the same kettle of blue vitriol, the white yarn would come out blue, the yellow would become a beautiful green. Some the early home made furniture can still be found. The four poster beds were made tall enough to permit a trundle bed to be rolled under during the day. If a room contained two beds with trundles under each, there was hardly walking space at night when they were drawn out. Records show that the ancestors of many of the families mentioned herein were in this vicinity before the Revolution, and many came soon after its close. It has been beyond my ability, both physically and financially, to delve as deeply as I would so much enjoy doing; however, it is amazing to know how many of you are direct descendants of the very first colonists who helped to establish this nation, from its very beginning; dating back to the 1600's, who gave of their toil, skill, their blood and their lives in founding this "Land of the Free and the Home of the Brave." It should inspire in us a pride and patriotism to be citizens of whom our forefathers could be proud. I hope some one of you will continue where I left off and record the future, as well as go to the old records of Virginia, Maryland, Pennsylvania, New Jersey, etc. You will be surprised to find familiar names among the first settlers and even members of the House of Burgesses.

Names of the earliest owners of land in this valley may be found on the book of Land Grants in the Harrison County Courthouse Record Room. However it is difficult to get the exact location because the survey maps designate lines running "from an oak tree so many poles to a chestnut," etc. Some border on the West Fork River or Robinson's Run and a "branch thereof." This stream was named for William Robinson who owned several thousand acres, reaching from Tenmile to Bingamon and to the river. His son, Major Benjamin, received a large tract around Lumberport as his pay for Revolutionary War service. In 1802, Basil Lucas (Rawley's grandfather), bought 22 acres from Philip Essex; also a certain tract about 1805 from Thos Chipps. In 1803, 70 acres on West Fork from Wm. Ruttley. 15 acres from Robt. McKean. 1807, 43 acres from Wm. Hall. 1821, 38 acres bordering the mouth of Robinson's Run along the river toward Lumberport, from Daniel Long. Another tract from Essex That would probably include what is now Poos Mine.

Rhodam Rogers received a land grant in 1798, between upper Robinson's Run and Jones' Run. In 1798, Lambert Flowers bought 309 acres from Wm. Robinson between Prospect Valley and Pigott's Run. One Wm. Flowers bought land from Robinson. In 1814, Henry and Elizabeth Coffman sold 225 acres to Daniel Long.

Frazier Heldreth (see Pigott genealogy), as early as 1790 owned land on the east side of Piggott's Run. His grave stone can still be seen marked with the initials just at edge of the forest near the base of Heldreth's Knob.

John Chalfant bought land from Basil Harvey on Robinson's Run near Harbert's in 1849. Then in October, 1852 he bought from Isaiah Harbert. In 1853, he acquired 127 acres on Bingamon from Peter Mason. In 1868 he bought two acres and 30 acres on Robinson's Run from Asbury P. Sturm. 50 acres from Dr. Caleb Flowers in 1875. In 1857 he bought 73 acres of John Tate.

Prospect Valley

(These first seven pages were told to Marshall W. Ogden by M. B. Bartlett in 1908.)

THE first records we have of Prospect Valley are when it was settled by William Robinson, who patented about all the land on Robinson's Run, Jones' Run and possibly part of Cunningham's Run. He is the ancestor of all the Robinsons now residing at Prospect Valley, Shinnston and surrounding country.

He sold off a large tract of land to Basil Lucas, the father of John D. Lucas, who was grandfather of William, Edward and Rawley G. Lucas. Basil Lucas built his log house on the hill between Prospect Valley and Lumberport where Luther Harbert later lived and Arthur Drummond lived until lately.

John Flowers, a well educated man, settled in the Valley and built a log house. He was the father of Jesse Flowers, who was the father of Dr. Caleb Flowers, and was of Irish descent. He with others constructed the only Indian fort ever built on Robinson's Run. This fort was erected near Limestone Spring up the ravine towards Pigott's Run from Robinson's Run, just above the Shinnston water works dam. The fort was below this spring some distance toward Robinson's Run. It was a two-story log fort with two rows of port holes. One upstairs and the other downstairs and was about forty feet square. The stockade was extended across water from the Limestone spring to give protection against siege by the Indians.

When the Indians were known to be in the neighborhood all the people sought protection in this fort where they remained until it was supposed to be safe for them to venture out. There is no record of any attack upon this fort by the Indians, although the people sought its protection on several occasions.

An Indian was seen prowling about this fort. He was fired on and wounded and ran into the laurel thicket where his pursuers dared not to follow him, but stood guard about the thicket for several days when a party ventured in and found the Indian dead. He was buried therein.

A slight encounter took place between the people of the fort and the Indians just up the ravine about two hundred yards from its mouth known as the Bartlet Branch. Some Indians were wounded but none killed and the Indians retired into the forest.

Another fort was built on Cunningham Run just above the Richardson farm. Another near what is now Haywood up on the flat near the ball ground. Another fort was just above Enterprise on the west side of the river on the Charley McIntire farm and near the two-story brick building owned by him. Another fort stood just above Hepzibah. All were very much alike in character of construction.

John Flowers engaged in the pottery business. having his kiln near his house below the Robinson's Run fort. His chief output was crocks, and besides selling to the settlers, he would occasionally build a boat at the mouth of Robinson's Run, load it with crocks, wheat, potatoes, etc., and float down the river to Pittsburgh to market.

His son, Jesse Flowers, was likewise well educated, a fluent speaker and influential man. Served in the Virginia Legislature and after the formation of West Virginia was a representative from Harrison County in the State Legislature.

The early settlers in Prospect Valley were William Robinson, John Flowers, Coffman, Pigott, George Lucas and others. They ground their corn on a hand mill made of two stones operating upon each other like burrs, about 20 inches in diameter, a hole in the center of the top in which the corn was placed, a hole in the outer edge of the top stone admitted a peg for a hand hold to turn the top stone on the other, the turning of the top stone crushing the corn as it passed between the stones and out as meal. This meal was made into a tough dough or cake placed on a shingle and set up at an angle of about 90 degrees in front of a rousing wood fire where it speedily became a Johnny cake. Later when wheat bread was made it was made into a cake of dough, placed in hot wood ashes, completely covered-up until baked, then it was raked out, the crust or burnt portions scraped off and the remainder was pronounced excellent.

The next means of grinding corn and wheat was by a mill turned by horse power. This mill was very much like the hand mill but was much larger and would serve for a whole neighborhood. The person owning and operating the mill made a small charge for grinding in the way of toll, and subsequently the water-grist and saw mills came into use and continued until about the year 1900 when steam roller mills were constructed and put into use by millers generally.

The first Ogden to reside on Robinson's Run was Nathan Ogden. He married Jane Duncan, who was a sister to Asbury Duncan, and resided with her people on a branch of Robinson's Run, known as Lemaster's Run, and the old log house stood a short distance back of the present church. After their marriage they resided with his father, Thomas Ogden, below Enterprise, for a short while and then moved to themselves in a little log house in the bottom below the Luther Ogden house, now Hutchinson. On the death of Thomas Ogden he gave, by will, this tract of land to his sons, Nathan and Samuel Ogden, and they with their respective families resided on it until the year 1855, when Nathan Ogden and his wife sold out to Samuel Ogden for $220.00 and conveyed their half of the 52 acres to Samuel Ogden, which deed is of record in the County Clerk's office of Marion County, in Deed Book No. 7, page 428. Nathan Ogden and his wife, Jane, acknowledged the deed before John H. Ogden and

Benjamin Martin, Justices of the Peace for Harrison County, Virginia, on the first day of January, 1855.

Nathan Ogden, his wife, Jane, Van B. Ogden, Thomas Jefferson Ogden and Sarena Ogden, their children, then moved on Robinson's Run on the share of the Duncan's land which fell to his wife, Jane, in the division of the estate. The house was a log cabin and stood on the left hand side of the road as you go up Lemaster's Run and was back of the church. Nathan Ogden followed farming, making staves, hoops, poles, etc., for about one year here and then he and his wife sold out their share of this estate to her brother, Asbury Duncan, and purchased, September 24, 1856, the tract of land about one mile from the mouth of Robinson's Run containing 29 acres and also a tract containing four acres from Eli Everson, as shown by Deed Book No. 51, page 415, in the County Clerk's office of Harrison County, West Virginia. The four-acre tract is now covered by the Shinnston water works dam. Nathan Ogden and his family immediately moved to this property and for many years operated the old water power grist mill at that place and also a water power saw mill on the extreme lower end of the place, using the four-acre tract as a reserve dam for water to operate these mills.

Nathan Ogden had but little education, but was a great reader and kept himself well posted on the affairs of his country. He opposed the election of Abraham Lincoln, believing that his election would mean war between the slave holding states and the North. He never owned a slave and did not believe in slavery. He was intensely religious and was a pillar in the Methodist Church of Prospect Valley. From his mill he purchased surplus wheat, corn, and other cereals, ground them in his mill and with the products of his saw mill built flat bottomed boats at the mouth of Robinson's Run at the old boat yard and shipped his products down the river to Pittsburgh.

He also manufactured staves, hoops, poles, etc., and included these products in his shipments down the river. He was reasonably successful financially, was a good natured fellow, enjoyed a joke, made his home the home of anyone in need, loaned his tools to his neighbors who never returned them, gave extended credit at his grist and saw mills, and enjoyed life, always industrious but never overworked himself or those who worked for him.

His first wife, Jane, died about 1868, leaving him and his daughter, Sarena, by themselves. He married —— Moore, who had two small children about 8 and 10 years old, over the objection of his children, and brought them to his house. She was a good woman and did all in her power to make his declining days comfortable. His daughter, Sarena, was dissatisfied with the situation and thought her step-mother's children were receiving undue consideration from her father and made her home with her uncle, Asbury Duncan, a great part of the time. She was then thrown into the company of Vina Shinn, afterwards the wife of Benjamin Mathews of Lumberport, who also stayed with Mr. Duncan.

While living in this situation he came up to Prospect Valley to his son, Van B. Ogden, one evening for some tools or instrument and was urged to stay over night, but he refused, insisting that he would have to return. He went home, had prayers as usual and retired apparently in his usual health. Some time in the night he complained that his dogs were making a fearful racket over in the mill race across the road and insisted on getting up and going over, to which his wife objected. He dozed off to sleep again and shortly awakened, and again insisted that the dogs were after something over in the mill race. He said he would get up and go to the door and look. He made a move and he relapsed into unconsciousnss. His wife called for help but no one could hear her, as the closest neighbor lived a half mile up the valley. She then sent her children, but it was dark and they were afraid and came back. She scolded them, they went again and informed the nearest neighbor, who then resided at the Drummond house. He sent some of his family down, got on his horse and rode to Nathan's son, Van B. Ogden, who hastened to his bedside, bathed his face in camphor, only to see him draw a few breaths and he was dead. He was buried in the Duncan graveyard, his widow returned to her people and Thomas Ogden continued to occupy the old homestead for a few years when he married Ella Varner, of Salem, and removed to that place to practice his profession of medicine. Sarena, the daughter, continued to reside at Asbury Duncan's home until she married Charles Daugherty, whom she had met on a visit to Reason Amos at Clarksburg.

Nelson Green Ogden is the authority for saying that Nathan Ogden was the essence of truthfulness and never told but one lie. He says that during the Civil War he, Nelson Ogden was a Southern sympathizer, came into the Valley, rode his horse to the lauel thicket and turned him out and went to his Uncle Nathan Ogden's to stay all night. While there some Yankee sympathizers heard of his being in the neighborhood and called at the house and inquired for Nelson Ogden. They were told by Nathan that he was not there and had not been there, while in fact he was in bed with his second son in an adjoining room. The soldiers went away satisfied, believing that what Nathan told them was the truth.

Prospect Valley Community

ROBINSON'S Run was named for the family of William Robinson who had land patents here as early as 1773.

William Robinson, born 1743, died October 18, 1815, married Margaret See Roach, widow, born 1745, died May 11, 1815. Their children, John, Benjamin, William II, James, Sarah, Mary, Elizabeth, Rebecca, Margaret and Catherine. McKinney was the son of James.

William R. was sheriff in 1788.

Benjamin married Mary Wilkinson May 19, 1785. Benjamin's daughter, Malinda, married George W. Boggess, parents of D. Marshall Boggess. Benjamin's son, John, married Rebecca Wamsley September 17, 1817. (See the Wamsley record.) Benjamin's son, David, married in 1809, Sarah Wamsley. John and Rebecca's children were David II, George, John, Caleb, Jesse, Ab, Dudley and Rebecca.

David II married Mary Cunningham, sister to Fred Cunningham. George, born November 24, 1821, died August 21, 1907, married August 27, 1844. Amelia Boggess, born January 15, 1824, died October 2, 1893. Rebecca married first Robinson, second Robert Mason. John married a Boggess, Abner married a Boggess, Dudley married Mary Mason, Caleb married a Boggess, Jesse married a daughter of Peter Hess.

John Deakins Lucas bought lands from William Robinson near the mouth of Pigott's Run.

The inter-marrying of the Robinsons, Coffmans and Harberts make up a greater part of the present population, while that of the Chalfants, Denhams, Lucases, and Bartletts have drifted elsewhere.

A School In Shinnston, 1860

GEORGE Fletcher, from Blacksville, Pennsylvania, taught several subscription schools before the free public school began.

My mother attended this one and boarded with a Fortney family. She remembered the name of every scholar after a period of seventy-six years. (1936.)

Christena Chalfant (Bartlett), my mother
Quillen Shinn, became a minister
Etta Sandusky, Mrs. Jesse Martin, mother of Attorney Hugh Martin
Mary Jane Davis
Alice Morris
Lummie Morris, Mrs. Bud Shinn
Clara Strickler, Mrs. Charles Watkins, just a little child
Mr. Haggerty, father of Mrs. S. O. Bond, Salem
Mr. Swiger
"Sis" Shinn, Mrs. Felix Martin, sister to Rev. Quillen Shinn
Augusta Fleming, Mrs. Wilkinson, sister to Bud F.
Nellie Fortney, Christena C.'s roommate
Solomon Chalfant, Christena's brother
Mary Long, daughter of Adam Long
Sarah Long, Mrs. Carder of Carder hotel
Lum Fortney (Sturm), sister to Gusta Wyatt
Bud Fleming, John Fleming, sons of Sol. Fleming
Pet Forman, Bates Davis' mother.

I have mother's McGuffey sixth reader she used in this school, 1857 edition.

Copied from a decayed and worm-eaten Sunday school class book dated 1858, Wesley Chapel, built in 1857, Prospect Valley, Harison County, West Virginia.

August, September and October, 1858.

Class No. I.

Robert Mason, teacher
Thornton Hardesty
Thomas Hardesty
William Chalfant—(married Mary Denham); parents of Arthur, Ellis, Dr. Martha, etc.
G. M. Sturm
V. B. Ogden
George Fortney
Brothers—M. Joe Crowl, Richard Crowl, father of Jackson, William Crowl, etc.
G. M. Fletcher, (subscription school teacher and cousin to John Chalfant, Sr.)
C. W. Sturm.

Class No. II.

Mary Denham, teacher, (sister to Robert and Martha)
Minerva Chalfant (married Edw. Lucas, parents of Charles F. Lucas)
Rachel Robinson
Mary Holders
Mary Ann Hardesty, (Mrs. Louis McIntire)*
Melvina Shinn, (lived with the Duncans, married Benj. Matthews, Jr.)
Martha Holder
M. J. Sturm
Sarah Bartlett, (Melville Bartlett's sister, married Jesse Martin).

Uncle Jesse and Aunt Sarah Jane are buried in the M. B. Bartlett lot at Shinnston cemetery.

Uncle Jesse and Aunt Sarah Jane had no children of their own, but they brought up a great many others, including one Will Hess, who later went to Urbana, Ohio, Charles and Jim Knox, of Shinnston, and later of Santa Monica, California.

---

*Mary Ann, daughter of James Hardesty, married A. P. Sturm.
Mary Ann, daughter of Frank Hardesty, married Louis McIntire.

Class No. III—1858

S. H. Dill, teacher—(may have been from Dill's Creek, Wood County)

Thornton Hardesty

Thomas Hardesty

Solomon Chalfant—(married Margaret McCoy, Pa., one son, Clarence O.)

Robert Denham—(father of C. C. Denham)

Washington Hardesty

J. W. Smith

J. M. Coffman

George Lucas—(brother to Mrs. Luther Harbert and uncle to Melville Bartlett, went to Redfield, Kansas)

Isaiah E. Hardesty

M. B. Bartlett—(married Christena Chalfant, parents of Homer, Henry, Lora, Nettie, Charles and Howard Bartlett)

Rawley G. Lucas—(father of John, Joseph and Basil H. Lucas)

Jesse Sprout

M— Baker (Mike)?

G. W. ——

Michael Baker was born with but one arm, lived at one time next to the stone church; was assessor of Harrison County about 1884. His father was a blacksmith. Joseph Baker made a "draw knife" for M. B. Bartlett in 1865, from the fine steel blade of a wheat cradle. It is still in our possession.

Class No. IV—1858

Martha Denham, teacher—(married Thornton Martin)

Mary Chalfant—(married Rawley G. Lucas)

Christena Chalfant—(Mrs. Melville Bartlett)

Rebecca Hardesty

Elizabeth Cavilier

Mary Nay

Louisa Shinn—(sister to Melvina)

L. C. Sturm
M. J, Sturm
A. Bartlett—(M. B. B.'s sister Hattie)

Class No. V

Asbury Duncan, teacher
John Nay
Jeremiah Chalfant—(father of Orville, Ola, Blanche and Wm., Jr.)
Jackson Crowl
Robert Chalfant—(son of John and Phoebe)
Harmon Shreve
George Lucas
Theodore Coffman

Class No. I—May, June and July, 1859

David Holder, teacher
William Chalfant
V. B. Ogden
Thornton Hardesty
Robert Mason—(married Rebecca Robinson, sister of David and George)
Silas Merrill
George W. Fortney
John O. Fortney—(father of Alf and Retta)

Class No. II—1859

Susan Allen, teacher—(wife of "Black" and mother of Tom Allen)
Mary Dunham
Minerva Chalfant
Martha Denham
Mary Ann Hardesty—(Mrs. A. P. Sturm)
Melvina Shinn—(Matthews, mother of Laura Matthews Coltrane)
Christent Chalfant—(aged 14)
Minerva Sturm
Martha Holder

Sarah Robinson—(sister to Dudley Robinson, married Marsene Rogers)
T. L. M.—(defaced)
Louisa Shinn

Class No. III—1859

Thomas Hardesty, teacher
Solomon Chalfant
Robert Denham
John M. Coffman—(father of Charles and Cora Hawker Hill)
Washington Hardesty
Jesse Sprout
—— Mason
George Ogden
Melville Bartlett
George Lucas
Rolly Lucas

Class No. IV—1859

Sarah Bartlett, teacher
Mary Chalfant
Rebecca Hardesty
Rebecca Sprout
Hannah Bartlett—(Hattie, died aged 17)
Jane Shreve
A. Coffman
M. J. Lindsey—(Jane)
B. Lindsey—(Bash)
Mary Davis—(daughter of Abe Davis)
Louisa B.—(Burns) ? "Dide" Sprout ?
Rebecca Davis—(daughter of Abe Davis)

Class No. V

A. W. Lindsey, teacher
Robert Chalfant
J. M. Lindsey—(Matt) ?
William Lindsey

Jeremiah Chalfant—(married Nettie Slocum March 13, 1879)
Wm. Sprout
I. M. Sprout—(Isaac)?
William Mason
E. Mason
H. T. Shreves
Theodore Coffman
John B. ——— (Burns ? Son of Jim and Nancy)
Arm Ashcraft—(son of Zeke)

Class No. ——(1864?)

R. G. Fortney, teacher
S. F. Fortney
Edgar Lucas—(married Minerva Chalfant)
A. R. Duncan
A. V. Duncan

Class No. II—(Date unknown)

Nancy Dawson, teacher—(mother of Kelly Dawson)
S. A. Ogden—(V. B. Ogden's sister)
Lib Flowers—(mother of Mrs. Edgar Harmer)
Amelia Cavilier
Mary Chalfant
M— Fortney
Dus ——— (torn away)

Class No. III—(Date unknown, probably 1870's)

Luther C. Harbert, teacher
Robert Chalfant
Elis ———
Ezra Duncan—(son of Asbury Duncan)
W. B. Ogden—(son of Van B. Ogden)

Class No. IV—(No date, 1870?)

V. E. Criss, teacher
Janey Ogden—(daughter of V. B. Ogden)
Bertha Harbert—(Luther's daughter, married Robert Rittenhouse)
M. B. Fortney—(Hiram Fortney's daughter Martha)

Class No. V—(No date, 1878 ?)

V. B. Ogden, teacher
John Duncan—(married Susan Michael, who was sister to Mrs. Albert Hardesty, went west) see Duncan geneology.
Arthur Chalfant—(son of Wm., went to Blackstone, Virginia)
Arthur Flowers—(A. O. Flowers, Clarksburg, son of Dr. Caleb Flowers)

Another Class No. I—(No date)

A. R. Duncan, teacher
V. B. Ogden
Solomon Chalfant
M. B. Bartlett
T. J. Ogden—(Thomas, brother to V. B. Ogden)

Class No. IV

David Holder, teacher
W. E. Pigott
Benjamin Flowers—(son of Basil)
Elmore Cavilier—(son of Silas, went to Missouri)
Robert Chalfant
Jackson Crowl
James Holder
J. A. Coffman
——— Richardson
——— Adkinson
James Moffett—(Captain in Civil War)

Class No. II—(May, 1864 ?)

Christena Chalfant, teacher
Mary A. Matthews—(Molly, sister to Benj., Jr.)
Sarah A. Young
Serena Ogden—(Daughtrey, Ina's mother)
Rebecca Cunningham
Martha E. Cavilier
E. Adkinson
Mary Chalfant

(Torn) nee Harbert
—— Holder
—— Coffman
—— Harbert

Class No. III—(Note, no date)

S. F. Fortney, teacher
Sarah V. Crowl—(Anderson—Sara Vesta)
Amelia Cavilier
M. A. Davis
T. J. Crim
C. J. Fortney—(Jack, grandfather of Prof. Roy McCuskey, President of Buckhannon College)
F. A. Flowers
Elizabeth Harbert
—— ah Fortney

Class No. IV—(No date)

Benj. Matthews, Sr., teacher
Wm. H. Cunningham
James Holder
S. Joe Crowl
James A. Moffatt
G. M. Adkinson
Dudley Moore
Benj. Flowers
—— Holder
—— Shreves
Elinor Cavilier

Nominations for Officers and Teachers—(No date)

Supt. A. R. Duncan
Assistant, V. B. Ogden
Secretary, S. F. Fortney
Librarian, Alva Duncan
Treasurer, James E. Lucas

Teachers:
1. B. G. Lucas
2. Nancy H. Dawson—(Nancy, mother of Kelly Daw-

son)
3. Luther Harbert—(also Class leader)
4. Virginia O———?

Class No. I—June, July and August, 1863

A. R. Duncan, teacher
V. B. Ogden
B. F. Coffman
Solomon Chalfant
Dudley Robinson—(married Mary Mason)
Thomas Ogden—(father of Wayman Ogden)
Thomas Hardesty
Harmon Shreves
William Chalfant—(grandfather of Guy, Helen and Fred)
J. E. Lucas
S. F. Fortney
Snyder ———
David Holder

Class No. III—July and August, 1863

Nancy Dawson, teacher
S. A. Ogden
Lib Flowers—(daughter of Dr. Caleb Flowers)
Amelia Cavilier
Mary Chalfant—(Lucas, mother of John, Joe and Basil)
M——— Fortney
Dus ———

Class No. II—June, 1863

Minerva Chalfant, teacher
Christena Chalfant—(Bartlett, aged 18)
Amelia Lucas—(sister to Rawley, married Wm. Nixon, parents of George Nixon and May N. McIntire)
Elizabeth McIntire
M. L. Robinson
Caroline Robbins
Sarena Ogden
Martha Holder
M. J. Sturm

H. W. Bartlett—(Hattie, Hannah, Unity, buried in Lucas cemetery)
M. Shinn
Mary Chalfant—(married Rawley Lucas)

Class No. III—(1863)

Sarah Jane Bartlett, teacher
Mary Chalfant
Rebecca Sprout
M. A. Davis
Amelia Cunningham
M. L. Cavalier
E. L. Coffman—(Mrs. Ferd Rogers)
Viola Flowers—(Mrs. Dr. Caleb Flowers)
L. J. Davis
Jane S———(Shreve ?)
Jane Lucas

Class No. IV—June, July and August, 1863

Benjamin Flowers, teacher—(brother to Dr. Caleb)
Marshall Pigott—(son of Milton Pigott)
Charles Flowers
Elmore Cavalier
Jerry Chalfant—(father of Orville, Wm., Jr., Ola, Blanche)
Robert Chalfant
George Holderman
Ezra Richardson
Sara Hester x—
Robert H. ———
John Duncan
Jesse Coffman
George Holder
L. M. Piggott

Class No. VI—(1863)

W. E. Piggott, teacher—(taught public school 54 years)
Harmon Shreves
Isaiah Moffatt

James Robinson
Henry Cunningham
John Medmala ?
Jesse Sprout

Class No. V—June, July and August, 1863

Francis Flowers, teacher—(daughter of Basil Flowers)
Martha Cavalier
Jam Shreves
L. J. Davis
R. J. Davis
L. C. Sturm
Salena Moore
M. J. Robinson
C. M. Shreve
Rebecca ———
Caroline ———
M. A. Davis
Aualiza Cunningham
Martha Davis

Class VII—August, September and October, 1863

George Holder, teacher
James Holder
Thomas Flowers
John Duncan
Wm. Taylor
Jesse Cunningham
J. R. Moffatt

Solomon Chalfant, Librarian for 1864, '65, '66, '67.
Class No. I, 1864, missing.

Class No. II—June and July, 1864

S. J. Bartlett, teacher
Christena Chalfant—(married Melville B. Bartlett Nov. 1, 1869)
Malvina Shinn—(married Benj. Matthews, Jr.)
Ortha Rogers
Nancy Fortney

Hannah Bartlett—(Hattie)
Jane Lucas—(married Luther Harbert)
Jane Sturm
S. Ogden
Nancy ———
B. ———

Class No. III—June, 1864

Minerva Chalfant, teacher—(married Ed. Lucas)
Mary Chalfant—(married R. G. Lucas)
Rebecca Davis
M. A. Davis
Rebecca Sprout
Martha Cowan
Viola Flowers—(sister to Drs. Arthur and Newton)
Jane Shreve
Sara Ma———
Martha ———
Francis Flowers

Class No. IV—1864

Thomas Hardesty
Elmer Piggott
Andrew Martin

Class No. V

Martha Holder, teacher
Francis Flowers
Elizabeth Flowers
Marietta Rogers—(Gore, mother of Ex-Gov. Howard Gore)
C——— Shreves
Martha Shreves
Jane Davis
Sarah Davis
Mary Davis
Sarah ———(James Sturm)

My mother told me that these Davis girls lived in a house just below where D. Albert Hardesty's barn now stands, later Erlen B. Hardesty's (1937). They were very fine quilters and also pieced many for Grandmother Chalfant. (I have two of them now). Once they were carrying a bundle of quilt pieces over the foot-log near Chalfant's (now George Coffman's and Seward Hardesty's barn) and they dropped the package in the water, and had a time rescuing them.

Civil War time no doubt is the reason for the absence of the men's class.

Class No. I—Missing

Class No. II—June, 1865

M. E. Ogden, Sr., teacher—(grandmother of Vera Robinson)
M. J. Sturm
Christena Chalfant—(aged 20)
Jane Lucas—(Harbert)
Serena Ogden—(Daugherty)
A. A. Lucas—(Mrs. Wm. Nixon)
M. J. Holder

Class III—June, 1865

Minerva Chalfant, teacher
Jane Shreves
Martha Cavilier
Mary Chalfant
Mary A. Davis
Frances Flowers
Lavernia Sturm
Jane Crim

Frances Flowers, "Frantie" was the daughter of Basil Flowers. Mr. Elmer (W. E.) Piggott just told me yesterday (June 29, 1937) that she was his childhood sweetheart. His name appears in the Sunday school class on the following pages. Basil Flowers went west and took his family to Holden, Missouri.

Class No. IV—1865

M. B. Bartlett, teacher—(also member of Home Guards, Civil War)
Benj. Flowers
Wm. E. Piggott
Thomas J. Flowers

Class No. V—1865

Thomas Hardesty, teacher
George Holder
James Holder
Marshall Piggott
George Allen
John Duncan
Albert Duncan
Wm. Allen
Elmore Cavalier
Albert Hardesty—(father of Erlen B. Hardesty)
Jefferson Crowl
Marion Pi— (Piggott ?)
Bazil Cr— (Crim ?)
   This page of the old record was badly decayed

Class No. I—May, June, 1866

Benj. Matthews, Sr., teacher
George Lucas
James Robinson
Jesse Holder
John M. Burns—(Jack, brother to Benj., Sara Cunningham, Louise Sprout, etc.)
Benj. Matthews, Jr.
Wm. Chalfant
M. B. Bartlett
A. R. Duncan
Wm. Mason
Hiram Nic—

See also three small class book still in fair condition containing classes from 1859 to 1868. I have copied the books into this one a little farther over.

Class No. V—May, 1866

Chrissie Chalfant, teacher
L. A. Flowers
S. J. Allen—(Thos Allen's mother)
M. A. Matthews
S. A. Exline
M. K. Matthews
L. J. Davis
M. H. Crim
(Torn) Coffman
—— Coffman
—— Coffman
—— Exline
—pia Flowers
—rissie Robinson
—— Hil—(Caroline Hill?)

The Exlines lived near Pigott's Run. Their farm became later a part of the Lucas estate. I remember seeing the old house, it was not far from R. G. Lucas' house on the hill.

Class No. I—1868

Geo. Fletcher, teacher—(also public school teacher)
S. H. Chalfant
P. G. Moffatt
Thos. Ogden—(V. B.'s brother)
M. B. Bartlett
B. Matthews
Elmer Piggott
G. M. Adkinson
A. R. Duncan
Benj. Matthews, Jr.

Class No. II—1868

Christena Chalfant, teacher—(aged 23, married Melville
  Bartlett, November 11, 1869)

E. Adkinson
E. E. Coffman—(Mrs. Ferd Rogers, parents of Ray, Bernard and Ada)
Ellen Ogden—(wife of V. B. Ogden)
M. M. Shinn—(Malvina Matthews)
Viola Flowers
Elizabeth Crim—(Betsy, wife of (1) —— Martin, (2) Burt Drummond)
Mary A. Matthews
Sarah Young
Sarah Fortney

Betsy Crim (Martin) was the mother of (1) Richard O. Martin, and (2) Jane Martin Drummond, wife of Wilford D. and mother of Francis, Arthur, Belle (Lucas), Amanda (Fortney) and Carrie (Mrs. Clay Davis).

Class No. III—May, 1868

Mary Chalfant, teacher—Mrs. Wm. Chalfant, Mary Dunham)
M. H. Matthews
Amelia Cavalier
Sarah A. Crowl—(mother of Ira Anderson)
Sara Exline
M. M. Rogers—(Marietta Gore)
Elizabeth Harbert
Lib Flowers
M— Adkinson
—— Baker

Class No. ——186—?

H. J. Fortney, teacher
S— Crowl—(Jackson)
Dudley Moore
James Moffatt—(father of George Moffatt)
G. M. Adkinson
Albert Shreves
Wm. T. Rogers
John Duncan

Albert Duncan
Marsh Piggott
——n Coffman

Class No. I—April, May and June, 1879

A. R. Duncan, teacher
F. W. Nay
M. B. Bartlett
A. O. Flowers
J. O. Duncan
Wm. Chalfant
Albert Duncan
A— Carder ?
Jamey Piggott
M. Cunningham

Class No. II—1879

V. B. Ogden, teacher
Ezra Duncan
E. N. Flowers
Albertus Ogden
Robert Chalfant
Jerry Chalfant
A.— Shreve
Benj. Harbert
An—Shreve
L—— ——
Basil — Boggess?
Ellis ——
James Lindsey
—— Chalfant

Class No. III—April, 1879

M. E. Ogden, teacher
Bertha Harbert—daughter of Luther and Jane Lucas Harbert, married Robert Rittenhouse)
A. M. Shreves
S. J. Ogden—(Janie ?)
Belle Flowers—(daughter of Dr. Caleb Flowers)
Belle Burns—(daughter of Jack Burns)

Class No. IV—April, 1879

— L. Hess, teacher
M. W. Ogden
Arthur Drummond
— W. Piggott
Ellsworth Ogden—(married Lillian Weekley, (1) Paul,
 (2) Ira and (3) Maxon, etc.)
(Torn) Piggott
Davy ——— (Robinson?)
W. A. Lindsey

Note the absence of Christena Chalfant Bartlett's name during the year of 1879. She was too busy at home looking after me about that time.

The preceding pages were copied from the mutilated class book which has fallen to pieces, I have enclosed the crumbled leaves in a box which can be kept in your Sunday school book shelves.

Going through these old names has brought to my memory many interesting stories of some of them, as was told to me from time to time by my beloved mother (Christena Chalfant Bartlett) who outlived the greatest number of them. She lived from October 26, 1845, to August 13, 1936.

I hope this book will be kept in the Wesley Chapel Sunday school bookcase, along with the three small brown class books which are still legible and should be preserved.

NETTIE BARTLETT COOPER
(One time pupil and teacher in the Wesley Chapel Sunday
 school.)

The following pages contain the names of the people of that same community who lived there during my own years there. From about 1880 to 1900.

If I have omitted any, will some one kindly fill them in?
Allen, Thomas—with the Lucas family, a half-brother to
 Albert E. Allen

Ashcraft, John—residence, the little house built for Francis Ashcraft, see below

Ashcraft, Martha Miller

Ashcraft, Curt

Ashcraft, Lillian

Ashcraft, Amanda

Ashcraft, Ernie—These children were our playmates. We had a great time arguing which baby was the prettiest, their cousin, Rosella or our little brother, Howard.

Ashcraft, George—Lived in the place now covered by the waterworks dam.

Ashcraft, Mrs.

Ashcraft, Bertha

Ashcraft, Romie

Ashcraft, Francis

Ashcraft, Vina Miller

Ashcraft, Rosella—Francis resided up the valley above our house. It was built in newly cleared land, especially for the bride and groom, Francis and Vina. Rosella was born there. Vina lost her wedding ring. I found it out in their yard almost buried.

Burns, Jack—The same house as above, but years earlier. At dam.

Burns, Mrs.

Burns, Belle

Burns, Annie

Burns, Benjamin—Resided in Ogden place below the dam.

Burns, Martha, first wife—Martha died there.

Burns, Jim—First on J. W. Flowers place above our orchard.

Burns, Nancy—Parents of Benj., Sarah Cunningham, etc.

Bartlett, Melville

Bartlett, Christena Chalfant

Bartlett, Homer A.

Bartlett, S. Henry
Bartlett, Lora
Bartlett, Nettie
Bartlett, Charles
Bartlett, Howard
Chalfant, John—Resided on the George Coffman farm just above Wesley Chapel, Prospect Valley.
Chalfant, Phoebe Conaway
Chalfant, William—See below.
Chalfant, Minerva—Married Ed Lucas, mother of Charles F. Lucas.
Chalfant, Solomon—Married Margaret McCoy; one son, Clarence, West Alexander, Pa.
Chalfant, Robert—Never married
Chalfant, Christena—Bartlett, died August 13, 1936, aged 91.
Chalfant, Mary—Mrs. R. G. Lucas
Chalfant, Jeremiah—See below
Chalfant, Johnny—Died at 13
Chalfant, William—Family:
Chalfant, Mary Denham
Chalfant, Arthur—In Blackstone, Va.
Chalfant, Russell
Chalfant, Ellis—Parkersburg, W. Va.
Chalfant, Dr. E. Martha
Chalfant, May—Mrs. Otto Reed. Reed was our first R. F. D. mail carrier.
Chalfant, Anna—Mrs. Rufus Ogden
Chalfant, Lloyd—Married
Chalfant, Willa Hoff
Chalfant, Helen
Chalfant, Guy
Chalfant, Fred
Chalfant, Jerry
Chalfant, Nettie Slocum—For whom I was named
Chalfant, Orville—They lived just below the church

Chalfant, Ola
Chalfant, Blanche
Chalfant, William
Conaway, Sant
Conaway, Belle Mason
Conaway, Minnie—William Coon
Conaway, Rose—Married Robert Swiger and is Mrs. Paul Hess's mother.
Conaway, Dove—Brand
Conaway, Sterling
Conaway, Fred
Conaway, Demas
Conaway, Mary
Crile, Caleb—Lived with John Chalfant, was as dear as a brother to us.
Coffman, John—Where James now lives, 1937.
Coffman, Achsah
Coffman, Benjamin
Coffman, Sheridan, Fillmore, Johnny—Alonzo's sons
Coffman, Luther
Coffman, Ida Cunningham—Daughter of Fred W. Cunningham.
Coffman, Dessie—Married Edward Richardson
Coffman, George—On the John Chalfant farm after Chalfants bought the Asbury Duncan place.
Coffman, Rosa Weekly
Coffman, Jessie—Seward Hardesty
Coffman, Aura—Earl Martin
Coffman, Lillian Weekly—Rosa's sister, married Ellsworth Ogden. Lived on the Luther Harbert place. Paul was born there.
Cunningham, Sarah—Burns
Cunningham, Samuel—Married first Dickie Drain, their children, Okey and Opal
Cunningham, Mary, Martha—Twins; Mary married Wilmer Martin; Martha married Wesley Dean.

Davis, Clay—Married Carrie Drummond
Dean, Wesley—Married Martha Cunningham
Daugherty, Ina—V. B. Ogden's niece
Drummond, Bert
Drummond, Betsy Crim—First wife
Drummond, Osadora—Second wife
Drummond, Fernando
Drummond, William—Second son
Drummond, Harrison
Drummond, Wilford
Drummond, Jane Martin—Sister to Richard O. Martin
Drummond, Francis—Killed by a train near Clarksburg
Drummond, Arthur—Married Maggie Sprout, their children were Ruby and Estelle
Drummond, Belle—Married Cliff Lucas, son of Frank
Drummond, Amanda—Lloyd Fortney
Drummond, Carrie—Clay Davis
Duncan, Ezra—Went west
Duncan, John—Went west
Duncan, Susan Michael—Sister to Mrs. D. A. Hardesty
Duncan, Forest
Duncan, Ray
Duncan, Albert
Duncan, Jennie—Wolford
Duncan, Clarence
Duncan, Ira
   Duncans all went to the middle Western States.
Fortney, John O.
Fortney, Alf
Fortney, Retta
Flowers, Dr. Caleb—Lived where Adolphus Shreves lives (1937)
Flowers, Naomi—Fortney
Flowers, Viola—Hess
Flowers, Libbie—First McIntire; second Hess. Mother of Mrs. Edgar Harmer

Flowers, Belle—Hustead, Sardis
Flowers, John
Flowers, Dr. Arthur O.—Clarksburg
Flowers, Dr. E. Newton—Clarksburg
Flowers, Jennie—Mrs. Meeks
Flowers, Kate
Flowers, Naomi (Sissie)—My childhood playmate, so full of fun. I visited her in Denver, Colo. in 1929.
Flowers, John
Flowers, Ida McIntire
Flowers, Ada—Another playmate and good friend
Flowers, Willie
Flowers, Charles
Flowers, Ida
Flowers, Howard
Haggerty, A. A.—Boother
Haggerty, Louise—Ashcraft
Haggerty, Lloyd
Haggerty, Leslie
Haggerty, Talbot
Haggerty, Chester
Haggerty, Grace
Haggerty, Lenna
Hardesty, D. Albert
Hardesty, Mary Michael
Hardesty, Emma—Married Ed. Rowan. Daughter Marguerite at Clovernook, Cincinnati, Ohio
Hardesty, Erlen
Hardesty, Florence
Hardesty, Edgar Waitman—Married Mattie Davisson
Hardesty, Elsie—Married Rev. Harry W. Flanagan
Hardesty, Anna—Married Chester Martin, first son Philip
Jones, Lewis—(Colored) A pretty good fellow but he just couldn't resist chicken roosts
Harbert, Benjamin, Sr.
Harbert, Mrs. Harbert

HISTORY OF PROSPECT VALLEY 37

Harbert, Samp.—One daughter, Margaret
Harbert, Benj., Jr.
Harbert, Janie Moore—Their children: May, Leota, Benj. III., Agnes
Harbert, Charles
Harbert, Frank
Harbert, Jerry
Harbert, Jacob
Harbert, Nathan
Harbert, Dora
Harbert, Mary
Robey, Martha—A niece
Harbert, Luther
Harbert, Jane—Lucas
Harbert, Bertha—Married Robert Rittenhouse
Harbert, George, Basil—Twins
Harbert, Emory
Lindsey, Matt—Matt carried the mail from Lumberport to Prospect Valley for several years. He would bring our mail to us on his return trip. Thus we had free delivery long before anyone else.
Lindsey, Frances—His sister
Lindsey, Ailsey
Lindsey, Ad
Lindsey, Bird
Lindsey, Columbia
Lindsey, Lou—Another playmate
Lindsey, Elmer
Lindsey, Loma
Lindsey, Rosa
Lindsey, "Doc."
Lindsey, Lottie—Burns
Lindsey, Ida
Lindsey, Vina—Marrie Thomas Ashcraft
Lindsey, Celia
Lindsey, Jim

Lindsey, Tom
Lindsey, Claude
Lindsey, Will ?
Lindsey, Thomas—Lived where the reservoir now is.
Lindsey, Mrs.
Lindsey, Etta
Lindsey, Flora
Lanham, John
Lanham, Mrs.—Harbert
Lindsey, Ad—Near Laurel Thicket on what was called the "Caleb Place."
Lindsey, Meade
Lindsey, William
Lindsey, Curt
Lindsey, Charles
Lindsey, Jennie
Lindsey, Myrtle
Lucas, Rawley
Lucas, Mary Chalfant
Lucas, John R.—Married Etta Willis
Lucas, Joe—Married Tillie Richards
Lucas, Basil—Married Mayme Hardesty
Martin, Richard O.
Martin, Jane Ashcraft
Martin, Russell—Married Bird Lindsey
Martin, Charles—Became the hero of the family and deserves a degree of honor for the way he has made a home for his parents and the younger children.
Martin, Wilmer
Martin, John
Martin, Cecil
Martin, Della
Martin, Albert
Martin, Mamie
Martin, Christena—Dawson
Martin, Nellie

Maulsby, Lawson—Lived on Luther Harbert place
Maulsby, Ella Harbert
Maulsby, Lorna
McIntire, Jeff—On old Lucas place mouth of Piggott's Run
McIntire, Mrs.
McIntire, Fletcher
McIntire, Fred
McIntire, Columbia—Burns
McIntire, Martha
McIntire, Lonnie
McIntire, John
Minnix, Andrew
Minnix, Ailse
Minnix, Mary
Minnix, Luther
Matthews, Laura—Daughter of Benj. Matthews, Jr., and wife Melvina Shinn Matthews
Moffatt, George
Moffatt, Mrs.
Moffatt, Peyton
Moffatt, Florida
Moffatt, Martha
Moffatt, Benny—With these children as my playmates at grandmother Chalfant's home, I have been blessed with happy memories of our innocent, wholesome fun. Benny was only a baby at that time, but the rest of us could climb the tallest tree for hickory nuts, mulberries, etc. Benny become Dr. Benjamin F. Moffatt.
Morgan, Laura—Sturm
Morgan, Gertrude—Winger
Morgan, Lillian—McClintock
Morgan, Ernest
Ogden, Van B.
Ogden, Ellen—Talkington
Ogden, William Burtice—Teacher

Ogden, Janie Shreve "Derry"
Ogden, Ellsworth—Married Lillian Weekly
Ogden, Emma—Married David Robinson
Ogden, Marshall W.—Married Lelia Hawker
Piggott, Milton
Piggott, Mrs.
Piggott, Benjamin
Piggott, Charles
Piggott, Lloyd
Piggott, Ellis
Piggott, Fletcher—Married May Harbert
Piggott, Arthur—Went west
Piggott, Clara—Married Homer Michael
Piggott, Janie—Married Adolph Shreve
Piggott, Flo—Married Otto Martin
Piggott, Herbert
Parsons, Mr. and Mrs. "Dick"—Lived in old Duncan House near the church
Quinn, Kitty—Lived with Robinson family
Robinson, James
Robinson, Jane—Hawker
Robinson, Davy—Married Emma Ogden
Robinson, Cecil—Married Frances Griffin
Robinson, Betty—Married Colfax McCarty, parents of Clyde, Omar, etc.
Robinson, Nellie
Robinson, Amos—Married Lorna Harbert
Robinson, Henry—Married Elsie Hardesty, daughter of James Hardesty
Robinson, Davy's family
Robinson, Emma—Ogden, daughter of V. B. Ogden.
Robinson, Wayman—Married Willa Robinson of Lumberport
Robinson, Vera—Teacher in Lumberport schools
Robinson, Lamar—Son of George
Robinson, Etta—Harbert, daughter of Seth Harbert

Robinson, Grace—Married Emory Cunningham
Robinson, Essel—Married Carma Mason
Robinson, Carl—Married Osie Mason
Robinson, Eva—Married Virgil Mason
Robinson, Lacie—Married Argyl Hess
Rice, John
Rice, Mrs.
Rice, Iva—One small brother
Rogers, Jesse—(Colored)—On the Caleb place across the run from Samuel Cunningham
Rogers, Linda
Rogers, Harriet, etc.
Shreve, John
Shreve, Mrs.
Shreve, Jacob
Shreve, Grant
Silcott, Nan—Lived at John Shreve's
Shreve, Adolph
Shreve, Jane—Piggott
Shreve, Daisy—Married Nathan Harbert
Shreve, Remmie—Lorna Maulsby
Shreve, Adolph—Second wife Allie Miller
Sturm, Rev. Asbury—M. E. South minister
Sturm, Mary Ann—Hardesty
Sturm, Verna—Snodgrass
Sturm, Jane—Atha
Sturm, Dora—Johnston
Sturm, Laura—Morgan
Sturm, Lee
Sturm, Ashby
Sturm, Ella—Married Wm. Hess, Wyatt
Sturm, Jessie—Married W. M. Hess, Mannington
Sturm, Blanche—Willison
Tucker, "Doc"; Tucker, Mary (Miller)—Housekeepers for John Chalfant after the death of Mrs. Phoebe Chalfant

Tucker, Delta
Tucker, Sherman
Sprout, Isaac
Sprout, Luisa—Burns
Sprout, Alden, Allison—Graduated with me in 1895 from Prospect Valley school. Erlen B. Hardesty, teacher.
Sprout, Maggie—Married Arthur Drummond
Sprout, Lora—Married Tal Haggerty
Sprout, Alden—Married Carrie, daughter of James Robinson
Sprout, Allison—Married Rosella Ashcraft, daughter of Francis and Vina Miller Ashcraft
White, Isaac—Cousin of Rosa Weekly Coffman
Wyatt, Dr. Z. W.—Lived in the Caleb Flowers and Adolph Shreve home. The doctor's office stood beside the highway below the house.
Wyatt, Dr. Z. W.—Second wife Augusta Fortney
Wyatt, Jackie, Jr.
Wyatt, John
Wyatt, Clyde
Wyatt, Leslie
Wyatt, ——— Daughter died young
Wyatt—Dr. Wyatt's mother lived there later.
Wyatt, Nellie—Married Robert Monroe
Wyatt, Russell—Died in Shinnston, never married.

The list of school teachers from the earliest years is very incomplete, and not in their regular order. John Robinson taught in a small dwelling house near the original Wm. Robinson home. Margaret Bowman, daughter of Jacob Bowman, taught one subscription school about 1850 in the log school house which was burned with the church in 1855. Verna Robinson and Christena Chalfant were two of the pupils about ten years of age. Margaret married John W. Boggess for his second wife. She was the mother of Arthur Boggess of Clarksburg. Moses Duncan.

Peter Goodwin and George Fletcher taught in the 1850's, also in the first free schools. These two men were cousins of John Chalfant, and boarded with him. Later teachers were Frank Martin, Felix Martin, R. G. Lucas (1869), Marshall Ice, —— Robinson, John Duncan, Newton Flowers, Russell McCarty in 1884. Alice Robinson in 1885, was my first teacher. She married Clay Hedges. Besta Denham, 1886; Burton D. Rose, 1887; Burtice Ogden three years; Nollie Taylor, 1891, was the first teacher in the new school house; Myrtle Moffatt, 1892; Marshall Ogden two years; Erlen Hardesty, 1895, when I graduated; George Martin, 1896. A photograph of that school group is mentioned on another page; Fletcher Pigott, 1897. There were summer subscription schools taught in the 1880's by Syene Denham, Emzie Brent (Fortney), and Edna Daniels, the latter a stepdaughter of Robert Denham.

The earlier teachers "boarded around." There were also some scholars from a distance who boarded in the neighborhood. Judge Charles W. Lynch and Otis Stout, of Clarksburg, stayed with the Bartlett family.

Copies of Three Small Brown Class Books

Wesley Chapel Sunday School. Copied by Nettie Bartlett Cooper, June 15, 1937.

Book No. I.

Class No. 2. August, 1858

Mary Denham, teacher (Mrs. Wm. Chalfant)
Minerva Chalfant, (Mrs. Ed Lucas)
Rachel Robinson
Mary Holder
Mary A. Hardesty
Melvina Shinn (Mrs. Benj. Matthews, Jr.)
Martha Holder
Minerva J. Sturm
S. Bartlett (Aunt Sarah Jane Martin)

Note: Mary Denham Chalfant was the mother of Arthur, Ellis, Russell, Dr. E. Martha, May Reed, Anna (Mrs. Rufus Ogden) and Lloyd Chalfant.

Minerva Chalfant was the mother of Charles F. Lucas of Shinnston, who has two sons, William and Van Buren Lucas. William has a daughter Barbara.

Mary A. Hardesty was the wife of Rev. A. P. Sturm, parents of Mrs. Wm. H. Hess (Jessie) Laura Morgan.

Mother of Mrs. Gertrude Winger, etc.

Class No. 2—May, 1859

Susan Allen, teacher
Mary Denham
Minerva Chalfant
Martha Denham (Mrs. Thornton Martin)
Mary A. Hardesty
Melvina Shinn (Lived at Duncan's)
Christena Chalfant (Bartlett, my mother)
Sarah Robinson (Sister to Dudley Robinson)
Minerva Sturm
Martha Holder
F. S. Mason
Louisa Shinn

Note: At the bottom of this page of the classbook is written in a mischievous boyish hand the following inscription: "The above named schollers have been very disobedient."

This misdemeanor was no doubt the cause for the petition which I have copied on the following page. Since its date coincides and the names also.

Notice that Melvina Shinn leads all the rest.

It was not such a serious matter as it seems, for they were all youngsters of the 'teen age.

May 8, 1859.

"Mr. F. Sturm:

"We, the undersigned members of the Sunday school at Wesley Chapel, looking upon you as a nuisance and a pest in the school; whereby your forwardness and impudence renders yourself perpetually contemptible to all sensible people.

"We, therefore, desiring to see the school orderly and prosperous, would very respectfully and in the spirit of Christian kindness, request you either to quit your officiousness in the school or to leave our society entirely and forever.

"Respectfully yours,

"M. CHALFANT (Minerva)
M. M. SHINN,   MARTHA DENHAM,
A. B. COFFMAN,   MARY DENHAM."

Sarah Robinson (Married Marcene Rogers, sister to Dud Robinson)
Ben. Coffman
Robert Mason
S. H. Dill
A. M. Lindsey
R. Denham
Sol Chalfant
S. Allen
J. B. Allen
Thos. Hardesty
M. Hardesty (Mrs. Lewis McIntire, Worthington)

Note: This paper was preserved in the diary of William Chalfant, eldest son of John and Phoebe Chalfant.

Class No. 2—June, July and August, 1863

Mary Chalfant, teacher (Mary Denham Chalfant)
Melvina Shinn
Hannah Bartlett (Aunt Hattie Bartlett, died, aged 16½, buried in Lucas cemetery beside her mother.)
Martha Holder
Minerva Chalfant
Serena Ogden (Ina Daugherty's mother)
Christena Chalfant (Mrs. Melville Bartlett)
Elizabeth McIntire

M. L. Robinson
Amelia Lucas (R. G. L.'s sister, married Wm. Nixon)
M. J. Sturm

No Sunday school on July 19th, quarterly meeting.

Class No. 2—May, 1864

Sarah Bartlett, teacher (Melville Bartlett's sister)
Sarah Jane Lucas (Mrs. Luther Harbert)
Hannah Bartlett
Christena Chalfant
Sarena Ogden
Melvina Shinn
Nancy H. Fortney
Elizabeth McIntire
Nancy Baker

Jane Lucas was half-sister to Elizabeth Lucas Bartlett who was the mother of Melville, Sara Jane and Hannah Bartlett. After the death of Elizabeth, Jane came to live with the three Bartlett orphans till she married. Then young Hannah Unity Bartlett died at the age of 16½ years, and Sarah married Jesse Martin, leaving Melville alone. One of the Holder families moved in with him till he married Christena Chalfant, November 11, 1869.

They lived on the farm between the reservoir and Lumberport, now owned by the John W. Flowers heirs. The house was burned since purchased by Flowers.

It was built by Wm. Sprout, Isaac Sprout's father, for Basil Lucas, uncle of Rawley G. Melville inherited it from Basil Lucas, his great-uncle.

Class No. 2—July, 1865

M. E. Ogden, teacher (Mrs. Van B. Ogden)
Christena Chalfant
M. J. Lucas
Serena Ogden (Sister to V. B. Ogden)
M. J. Holder
Amelia Lucas (Nixon, mother of George Nixon and May
    Nixon McIntire.)
M. J. Sturm

Class No. 2—1866

Basil L. Flowers, teacher
Jane Lucas (Harbert, mother of Geo. and Basil Harbert, twins)
Hattie Harbert
Mary Holder
Caroline Hill
Mary Chalfant
Mary Mathis
Elizabeth Coffman
Viola Flowers (Daughter of Dr. Caleb Flowers)
Martha Cavilier
Minerva Chalfant

Dr. Caleb Flowers lived on the opposite hillside from the church. Now owned by Adolphus Shreve, 1937.

His family:

Flowers, Mrs. Naomi—Fortney
Flowers, Dr. Caleb
Flowers, Viola (Married Hess)
Flowers, Elizabeth (Married McIntire)
Flowers, John (Married Ida McIntire)
Flowers, Dr. Arthur O. (Married May Piggott, daughter of Elam Piggott)
Flowers, Dr. E. Newton
Flowers, Belle (Married Hustead)
Flowers, Jennie (Married Grover C. Meeks)
Flowers, Kate (Married A. Green)
Flowers, Naomi (Sissie) (Married Satoris Long, Clarksburg, now in Denver, Colo.)

Class No. 2—May, 1867

Chrissie Chalfant, teacher (Christena)
Mary A. Mathis (Molly)
Sarah Young
Serena Ogden
Martha Cavilier
E. Adkinson

Mary Chalfant (Mrs. Rawley G. Lucas)
Rebecca Cunningham
Martha Holder
Jane Harbert (Wife of Neaf Harbert)
Elizabeth Fortney
Phoebe Stackpole (Lived somewhere near the mouth of Robinson's Run)
Mrs. Jane Harbert (Wife of Luther Harbert)
Elizabeth Coffman (Mrs. Ferd Rogers)

Elizabeth was the only sister of John Coffman's thirteen sons.

Martha Cavilier was the daughter of Silas and Nancy Nay Cavilier and she married Fred Burns, son of James and Nancy Burns. Martha had a brother Elmore Cavalier. They all went to Holden, Johnson County, Missouri.

Fred Burns lived in the little house to the left of Dr. Caleb Flowers (later Adolph Shreve). The house was later moved farther down, opposite V. B. Ogden's. John W. Flowers also occupied that house at one time.

Class No. 2—May, 1868

Chrissie Chalfant, teacher
Ed Adkinson
Sarah Young
S. A. Ogden
Cath Fortney
Viola Flowers
Melvina Shinn
Mary A. Matthews (Sister to Benj., Jr.)
Amelia Lucas (Sister of Rawley G. Lucas)

Christena Chalfant was nicknamed "Chrissie" by Mary Jane Davis, of Shinnston, while attending school there. See page 6.

Book No. II
Class No. 3—1858

S. H. Dill, teacher
Solomon Chalfant (Son of John Chalfant)

Robert Denham (Son of Claiborne Denham)
Washington Hardesty
J. W. Smith
J. M. Coffman
George Lucas (Brother to Elizabeth Lucas Bartlett and
    half-brother to Jane Lucas Harbert)
Isaiah Harbert
M. B. Bartlett
G. W. Ogden
Rolly Lucas
Jesse Sprout
Mike Baker (One armed man, son of the blacksmith)

This class roll seemed to have been rewritten into this from the older book.

Robert Denham was wounded in the Civil War. Had a stiff knee ever after, till in his old age was struck by an automobile while crossing the street from his furniture store in Fairmont, West Virginia. He badly injured his good knee. He discovered that the old stiff knee had been knocked loose and was all right again.

(He told me this himself, and I also had known he had been lame before, and saw him well afterward. N. B. C.)

Class No. 3—May and June, 1859

Thomas L. Hardesty, teacher
Solomon Chalfant
Robert Denham
Washington Hardesty
J. M. Smith
J. M. Coffman
George Lucas
Isaiah Harbert (Great-grandfather of Essel Robinson, Carl
    Robinson, Gracie Cunningham, Eva Mason, and
    Lacie Hess)
M. B. Bartlett
George Ogden
Rawley Lucas

Wm. O. Ma ?
Jesse Sprout
Dudley Robinson
Wm. C. Mason
B. F. Coffman
William Mason

Isaiah Harbert married Orpah Shinn, daughter of Clement Shinn.

Class No. 3—May, June and July, 1864

Minerva Chalfant, teacher
Mary Chalfant (Mrs. R. G. Lucas)
Mary A. Davis
Rebecca Sprout
Martha Cavilier (Daughter of Silas Cavilier)
Viola Flowers
Jane Shreves
Sarah Martin
Verna Sturm
Rebecca Davis (Daughter of Abe Davis)
Elizabeth Coffman (Rogers, mother of Ray Rogers)

Class No. 3—June, 1865

Minerva Chalfant, teacher
Martha Cavilier
Jane Shreves
Mary Davis
Mary Chalfant
Frances Flowers (Daughter of Basil Flowers)
Jane Crim
Vereney Sturm
Mary Chalfant
Martha Cavilier

Class No. 3—1866

Seth Fortney, teacher
S. V. Crowl (Sara Anna Vesta Anderson, mother of Ira Anderson)
Amelia Cavilier

M. A. Davis
C. J. Fortney
T. I. Crim
F. A. Flowers (Frances ?)
Elizabeth Harbert
Sarah Fortney
Sarah Davis

Class No. 3—1867

Minerva Chalfant, teacher
Viola Flowers
Mary F. Adkinson
Sarah H. Crowl
Amelia Cavilier
Frances Flowers
F. E. Adkinson (Fanny ?) A very pretty girl
Sarah Exline
M. H. Mathis
June Crim

Fanny Adkinson and Jacob Crowl (son of Richard) were crack spellers; they were never known to be "turned down" in a spelling match.

There was a woman named Liz Drain who claimed to go into trances, at the church, and someone would always have to carry her home. Once they decided to play a joke on her. When they came to the foot log which crossed Robinson's Run, Jacob Crowl said, "Let's duck her in the water." She a once began to squirm and was awake in no time.

Class ———. Neither dated or numbered but followed the preceding page, evidently 1868.
Mary Chalfant
E. A. Flowers
M. H. Adkinson
E. M. Adkinson
M. A. Cavilier
Sarah Exline

M. C. Mathis
C. J. Exline
E. J. Exline

End of second small brown book.

Grandfather had a store in Prospect just after the Civil War, mother, his daughter Christena, worked in the store a great deal, so did Melville Bartlett. There no doubt, was where their long courtship began. Grandfather always was in favor of him.

Once he and another young man came to see mother and Aunt Mary. He was one that grandfather didn't care for as a son-in-law. So he went to the door and said, "Gals! What time will I get started to Baltimore in the morning?" The young men left immediately. The following week when he returned, and they were in the store, grandfather said, "I didn't mean that for you, Melville, its all right for your to come."

Book No. III.

Class No. 1—May, 1859

Robert Mason, teacher
George Fletcher, assistant
Thomas Hardesty
Wm. Chalfant
F. M. Sturm
V. B. Ogden
George Fortney
A. R. Coffman
Richard Crowl (Married Amy Cavilier)
C. W. Sturm
S. H. Dill
John Fortney
C. B. Flowers (Dr. Caleb Flowers, father of Drs. A. O. and Newton F. of Clarksburg)
A. R. Duncan

Note: George Fletcher was teaching a subscription school in a small school house built by John Chalfant on his own land. The course of the stream has been changed since, and the spot holding the building does not look the same. (See map.)

My mother has told me many interesting stories concerning these days of both Sunday school and the subscription school. The building across the road was for the older boys. Peter Goodwin and George Fletcher each taught there. I have no date for Goodwin, but George Fletcher taught, at least in 1859. Also the free school in 1868.

He told the boys not to talk or whisper. He left them on their honor while he was over in the regular school house.

On one occasion Sol Chalfant and Robert Denham had a wrestling match, but neither they nor any of the other boys spoke a word during the time. Thus they could truthfully report to the teacher that no one had talked during his absence.

George Fletcher taught several terms of school there, also after the public schools were established.

He taught there as late as 1868, after the other school house was built.

The little Chalfant school house was later moved to Prospect. It was located beside the main highway on the run, facing down stream. Next to it was John and Sol Chalfant's store.

Laura Morgan and her family lived in it as I first remember it. Later Sarah Cunningham with her children, Samuel, Martha and Mary.

Class No. 2—May, 1859

Mary Denham, teacher (Mrs. William Chalfant)
Minerva Chalfant (mother of Chas. F. Lucas)
Mary Holder
M. A. Hardesty
Melvina Shinn
Martha Holder

Martha Denham
Mary Chalfant
M. J. Sturm

The old church was burned about 1855. The school house was only about 40 feet away, so it burned also.

The citizens then decided to build a church that "could not be burned." Hence the present stone one. Everybody volunteered their services, gathering stones from the surrounding fields. Mr. Levi Kennett was a stone mason and was employed to build it. He lived during that time in the former Chalfant store building. He had one very fat little boy. The entire cost of the church did not exceed $900.00. Mr. Kennett had also built a similar church in Barracksville, Marion County, in 1854, although it was much smaller. It has been enlarged since.

Rev. Gordon Battelle dedicated the church in 1857. Rev. Thomas H. Trainer was the pastor.

Class No. 3—1859.

S. H. Dell, teacher
Solomon Chalfant
Robert Denham
Washington Hardesty
J. W. Smith
*J. M. Coffman
George Lucas (Half brother of Jane Harbert—Mrs. Luther Harbert)
J. E. Boggess (Ed.)
M. B. Bartlett

July 12, 1937. Up to this writing I have not been able to find out anything about anyone named Dell.

Class No. 4—May, 1859

Sarah Bartlett, teacher
Mary Chalfant (transferred to No. 2)
Christena Chalfant (transferred to No. 2)

---

*John Marshall Coffman, son of John and Achsa, was the father of State Senator Charles G. Coffman and Cora Hawker Hill.

Rebecca Hardesty
Elizabeth Cavilier, removed (Amy Crowl?)
Mary Nay, removed
Louisa Shinn (lived at A. R. Duncan's)
L. C. Sturm (transferred)
M. J. Sturm (transferred to Class 2)

Class No. 5—May, 1859

A. R. Lindsey, teacher
John Nay (removed)
Jeremiah Chalfant
Jackson Crowl (removed)
Robt. Chalfant
Mason Lindsey
William Lindsey
William Mason
T. E. Coffman
Harmon Shreve
Ellis Mason
William Sprout
Isaac Sprout (married Louisa "Dide" Burns)

A List of the Officers and Teachers—1859

B. L. Flowers, Superintendent
Robert Mason, Assistant
C. B. Flowers, Secretary (Dr. Caleb)
A. R. Duncan, Treasurer
W. M. Chalfant, Librarian

Teachers:
Class 1   D. Holder
Class 2   Susan Allen (Tom's mother)
Class 3   Thos. Hardesty
Class 4   Sara Bartlett
Class 5   A. W. Lindsey
          V. B. Ogden
          V. Sturm
          — Duncan
          R. Duncan
          B. L. Flowers

Basil Flowers and Silas Cavilier took their families to Holden, Missouri.

Silas Cavilier had a brother out there named Tim, who married an Indian and had a family of children. Once an Indian tribe made an attack, killing all the white men, but spared the women and children. He was one of the victims. (This was told to me (1937) by his grand-nephew, Wm. A. Crowl, son of Richard and Amy Cavilier Crowl.)

Class No. 1—Organized in May, 1859

David Holder, teacher
George Fortney
F. M. Sturm
V. B. Ogden
Thos. Hardesty
A. B. Coffman
J. O. Fortney
B. Coffman
S. H. Dell

Silas Cavilier married Nancy Nay. Their children were (1) Martha C., who married Fred Burns, son of James Burns, and (2) Elmore.

They built and lived in the house in Prospect Valley later owned by V. B. Ogden, then by John or Francis Ashcraft.

Class No. 2—1859

Susan Allen, teacher
Mary Denham
Sarah Robinson
Edith Sprout
Martha Denham
Melvina Shinn
Minerva Chalfant
Christena Chalfant
M. J. Sturm
M. A. Hardesty

Susan Allen, first wife of "Black" Allen, and mother of Tom Allen, who later made his home with the Lucas family.

Mrs. Allen was a sister to Fleming Jones, who at one time lived in the John Flowers house. He and his entire family died there with diphtheria.

M. A. Hardesty became Mrs. Louis McIntire, Worthington, W. Va.

Class No. 3—1859

Thomas Hardesty, teacher
Robert Denham
Solomon Chalfant
J. M. Coffman
Washington Hardesty
George Ogden
Jesse Sprout
W. M. Mason
Claiborne Denham

The Denham family lived across the river at the mouth of Robinson's Run.

Class No. 4—1859

Sara Jane Bartlett, teacher
Minerva Chalfant
Hattie Bartlett
Rebecca Hardesty
Bash Lindsey
Meda Coffman
Jane Lindsey
Louise Shreves
Mariah Davis
Jane Davis
Rebecca Sprout

Class No. 5—1859

A. W. Lindsey, teacher
W. M. Sprout
Jeremiah Chalfant

Robert Chalfant
Wm. Mason (transferred)
Ellis Mason
Madison Lindsey (Matt)
Wm. Lindsey
Thad Coffman
H. Shreves
Isaac Sprout
John Prunty

May 31, 1863

B. L. Flowers, Superintendent
David Holder, Assistant Superintendent
V. B. Ogden, Secretary
Edmond Lucas, Treasurer
Melville Bartlett, Librarian
J. E. Lucas Treasurer
  Teachers:
A. R. Duncan, 1st Class
Mary Chalfant (Denham) 2nd Class (Mrs. Wm. Chalfant)
S. J. Bartlett, 3rd Class
H. McIntire, 4th Class
Caroline Robbins, 5th Class
Thos. Hardesty, 6th Class
Thomas Ogden, 7th Class

Basil Flowers lived in the house where Isaac Sprout later lived, and in 1937 John Lucas used the same place for his riding school, across the road from the reservoir. His mother was "Poppy" Lucas, sister to William, Basil and George Lucas.

Class No. 1—1868

George Fletcher, teacher
S. H. Chalfant
J. G. Moffatt
T. J. Ogden
M. B. Bartlett

Benj. Matthews, Jr.
Wm. E. Piggott, Piggott's Run
G. M. Adkinson, Robinson's Run
A. R. Duncan (father of John, Albert and Ezra)
Benj. Matthews, Sr.

Benj. Matthews, Jr., married Melvina Shinn. They had one daughter, Laura, who married Nat Coltrane. Benjamin later had a second wife and family.

Laura Matthews was vivacious and loved a joke. Once she wrote to the Clarksburg Telegram saying that Belle Drummond would teach a summer school at Prospect Valley.

The "Telegram" worded it thus: "Miss Belle Drummond will teach a graded school at Prospect Valley. Address her as above for particulars." I can see Laura yet. How she laughed when see saw it. A few days afterward Belle received a bill for the advertisement. Laura was staying with her cousins, the V. B. Ogden family at the time.

Belle is the daughter of Wilford and Jane Drummond. She married Clifton Lucas, son of Frank, who was the son of Thomas, son of William, brother of George and "Uncle Basil" Lucas.

Class No. 2—1868

Chrissie Chalfant, teacher (Mrs. M. B. Bartlett)
D. E. Adkinson
E. E. Coffman (Mrs. Ferd Rogers)
Ellen Ogden (Mother of Marshall W. Ogden and Emma
    Robinson)
M. M. Shinn
Mary A. Matthews
Viola Flowers

Mary A. Matthews, better known as Molly, later lived on the Lumberport Hill road towards Lambert's Run. She was a great weaver of rag carpets. She did several for my mother. Once she sent brother Charles and me on horseback to take materials to her. We stayed all day, and it was quite a thrill to eat dinner with them. We were very small and mother became uneasy when we were gone so long. We thought we had to stay because they invited us. She and her sister Elizabeth lived together They were daughters of Benjamin Matthews, Sr.

Class No. 3—1868.

Mary Chalfant, teacher
M. M. Matthews
Amelia Cavilier
Sarah Crowl (married Marcene Anderson, one son, Ira)
Sara Exline, Piggott's Run
T. Jane Crim
Elizabeth Adkinson
Emily J. Exline

Adkinsons lived somewhere near the mouth of Robinson's Run. They with the Youngs had been forced to flee from the southern part of the State during the Civil War. The Adkinsons finally went back, but Sarah Young married Daniel Mason. (See Mason genealogy.)

Class No. 4—1868

H. J. Fortney, teacher
Jackson Crowl (Upper Robinson's Run)
Jas. A. Moffatt (Robinson's Run)
Albert Shreves (Jones' Run)
Wm. Rogers (Robinson's Run)
John Duncan (Duncan's lived on the right of the highway about half way between Prospect Valley and the top of the Peora Hill)
Albert Duncan
Marshall Piggott.
Jap. N. Coffman

Class No. 5—1868

C. B. Flowers, teacher (Dr. Caleb Flowers)
Charles L. Fortney
Geo. R. Fortney

George Moffatt
*Geo. Coffman
Black Crim (On Peora Hill)
Wm. Allen (Lumberport)
Thos. J. Crim (Bingamon)
Luther Piggott
Jas. A. Chalfant (son of Wm. and Mary "Denham" Chalfant)
—— Shreves
Jeremiah Chalfant

Class No. 6—1868

S. A. Young, teacher
E. A. Rogers (Robinson's Run)
Sarah Cumberlage (Robinson's Run)
Malinda Exline (Piggott's Run)
Mary E. Matthews (Robinson's Run)
Mandy Harbert
S. N. Shreves (Piggott's Run)
—— Shreves (Piggott's Run)
Fanny V. Shreves (Piggott's Run)
Lucy Ashcraft (Piggott's Run)

Class No. 7—1868

Jos. Exline, teacher
Newton Crim
F. Mathews
Alpheus Drain (Bingamon)
Enos Adkinson (Robinson's Run)
Emery Piggott (Piggott's Run)
Benj. Harbert, Jr.
Samp. Harbert
John Flowers
Thos. J. Allen (Lumberport)
F. Ashcraft (Bingamon)

---

*George Coffman married Rosa Weekly and became the owner of the John Chalfant farm. Chalfants went to the Asbury Duncan farm, which they later sold to Luther Piggott.

Newton Cumberlage (Robinson's Run)
Elmore Coffman
John Chalfant

Class No. 8—1868

Catherine Fortney, teacher
E. J. Exline (Piggott's Run)
M. M. Rogers (Robinson's Run)
Elizabeth Harbert
Libbie Flowers
M. H. Mathews
Crissie Robinson

Total enrollment for 1868—78.

S. H. CHALFANT, Librarian.

Mother told me (in 1935) that she could remember her father taking her to Dr. Johnny Flowers when she was five years old (1850). He carried her on horseback. I'll put it in her own words:

"As we went down the road (from the now George Coffman farm) father reached up and pulled off a brilliant red leaf from a tree just below our house. I kept it in my hand the entire trip. Inside the Dr. Flowers house (the one where the stone cellar still remains) there were two four-poster beds, between the beds was a bureau. On top of it were two large glass boxes with artificial flowers inside them, one at each side of the bureau. There was also something sitting between the boxes, but I can't quite remember what it was, it may have been a clock."

There have been five generations of doctors from Dr. John to the present time: Red-headed Jesse, who lived on the R. G. Lucas hill; Caleb lived in Prospect Valley, his two sons, Drs. Arthur O., and Newton E. in Clarksburg, the latter's son Earl N. Flowers, also in Clarksburg.

When grandfather, John Chalfant, came here from Monongalia County in the early 1840's, his farm was a virgin forest in which could be found arrowheads and an occasional tomahawk. The entire low valley was a magnicent sugar maple grove. They made maple syrup and many pounds of sugar.

1880 to 1900

Some of the most interesting activities during these twenty years were the literary society, spelling bee, subscription "writing schools," singing schools and grammar school.

Mr. Dudley Moore was the best authority on grammar, and was the finest instructor in the county. He could dissect Harvey's Grammar and build it all up again.

The first singing schools I can remember were taught by Thaddeus Hardesty, son of Joseph Hardesty, at Wyatt, and another by Mr. Ellis Mason. I was too young, however, to attend them, but I can still hear the do re me fa's and the ring of the tuning fork.

Then Ezra Duncan was a good song leader, too; he worked so hard trying to teach us youngsters the Children's Day songs. His voice was very nasal.

We were once battling with

"Hear the pennies dropping,
Listen as they fall,
Every one for Jesus,
He will get them all."

He said "No! No! Now try again this way," and he sang it again. My sister Lora, who was then about seven, lost her patience and started right in to sing it alone, through her nose, imitating him. This raised a rousing burst of laughter from the crowd of grown ups.

Later singing instructors were Essel Robinson and Ulysses E. Martin. These were the ones I attended and it was here we had drilled into us the theory of reading at sight. We had some happy times there; we had the singing school in the church.

The others were in the school house.

Ellis Chalfant was our penmanship teacher.

The only one I attended was taught by Douglas Robinson of Lumberport (a brother of Alice Robinson Hedges). He taught me in the Upper school, located near Lamar Robinson's home.

I was very young, but begged my parents to let me go too, along with Homer, Henry and Lora. They said I should not go unless I would learn to write with my right hand. This was a hard thing to promise, because I was left-handed in everything. But when I found that they positively wouldn't let me go otherwise, I finally consented. And I lived up to my promise and I learned to write with my right hand. So from that day to this, I can write with either hand, but I use my left hand in everything else. I do all my writing with my left hand, unless I am in some public place where people are looking on.

The Friday Night literary societies met alternately at the upper and lower schools for a long period.

These meetings gave the young man, both bashful and otherwise, the opportunity to say "May I see you home?" And the shy blushing maiden would say "Yes" or "No" as she saw fit.

Sometimes when a young swain would be calling on his girl, he would find his saddle missing when he came out to go home, or sometimes the horse would be gone too.

Once a saddle was hidden in A. P. Sturm's barn under the hay for six months, just because the perpetrator was too scared to tell.

These pranks were not always played by boys either, it was a girl who hid the saddle.

And once upon a time, don't tell anybody, Ada Flowers and I unhitched a horse from somewhere in the town of Prospect and led it up the moonlit road, almost to Grandfather Chalfant's house (on the Duncan place toward Peora). We tied it to the fence and went on.

Blanche Sturm will not mind now if I tell, for she told us years afterward that she hid that saddle in her father's barn. It belonged to her big sister's beau.

Chalfant's Grove

THE beautiful beech trees, most of which are still standing (1937) on the rolling hillside of my Uncle William Chalfant's farm, made an ideal picnic and all day meeting ground.

Many basket-meetings and Children's Day programs were held there. A speaker's platform and seats made of new sweet smelling lumber, and long tables for the dinners made an inspiring picture. Uncle William always had several hives of bees, and once we suddenly heard the musical hum of hundreds of bees, and they had made an attack on someone's dinner basket which held some sweets which attracted them. There was a bit of excitement till the basket was hurried down over the hillside away from the people. I didn't get to see how they got rid of the bees.

On those great smooth beech tree trunks can still be seen hundreds of names and initials. Some are far above the ground, showing how much the trees have grown since some of the names were cut. The beautiful home in which that family grew up was burned a few years ago.

Another picnic ground which was used a few years we named Beechwood Park. It was a smaller place but very pretty, was in a low nook just below where the reservoir now is. It was spoiled when the oil well was drilled right in the center of it.

We had a nice large platform on which was placed our organ and seats for the choir and those who were to speak "pieces."

That was in the horse and buggy day.

I was the smallest girl in Miss Vesta Denham's school. She would sometimes let me ride on behind her as far as our road. She rode a white horse, he didn't like to carry double. Once just as we started up that hill just below

Prospect Valley he started to run away. I yelled with every jump he made. Miss Denham said, as we neared the top, "Hold tight to me." She reached around and got hold of my left arm, and without telling me she leaped from the horse's back. And that nasty horse stopped instantly, turned around and looked at us.

A badly bumped nose which hurt me several days was our only damage. I never rode him again.

The older boys and girls coming along behind heard my yells, and the horse's galloping feet, and came running. They were brothers Homer and Henry, Russell Martin, Arthur Drummond and Will and Curt Lindsey.

Vesta Denham was the daughter of Dr. James Denham, across the river from Gypsy.

There was a splendid baseball ground in the field across the highway from the Laurel Thicket (later the reservoir). Many were the games there that were just as thrilling as any big league teams could produce.

We would sit over in our own field across the ravine through which flowed Robinson's Run and watch the game.

We could easily hear the cheering and the crack of the ball hitting the bat from our own front door yard, although too far away to see.

On quiet summer evenings we could sit there and hear the music of the Shinnston band floating up that valley. They would play out-of-doors, and we were three miles away.

The ball ground was in the same field where many years before had been the home of Dr. Johnny Flowers, where he practiced medicine and taught loud school. The stone cellar wall can still be seen; it is out near the steep bluff where the run crosses under the highway and into the lake. Johnny F. was the father of "Redhead" Jesse and grandfather of Caleb. His home was two one-room log houses about 30 feet apart. He taught loud school in the big kitchen.

This same ground is, at the time of this writing, being used by John R. Lucas for a riding school.

We thought we had reached the peak of civilization when the telephone party lines were established. No phone could ring without everybody running at break-neck speed to listen in.

Then some evenings we would have an entertainment over the telephone. Once Carl Robinson and Gilmer Cunningham tried a violin duet. They could not hear each other, but kept together pretty well.

Mr. Wm. Cunningham, who was then quite old, said "let me play one." Then we all listened quite a long time, not hearing a sound. Finally he spoke again saying, "How was that?" We had not heard him because he had hung up his receiver while he played.

That was in the year 1900. One great subject of conversation that year was whether the twentieth century began January 1st, 1900, or January 1st, 1901. We would always stop if anyone spoke up and said: "Will you please let me have the line a minute?"

Van B. Ogden was postmaster, merchant, and shoemaker. It was always a thrill when father would say: "Well, children, next time you go over to Prospect, go in and get your measure taken for your new school shoes."

The Flood of 1888

IT COULD not reach our community, but we all went over to Lumberport to see the high water. We could not get to the foot of Harter hill. We could see the tops of chimneys sticking out of the water. Then just the roofs of the homes of "Black Sam" and Gordon Cambric were nearest to where we stood. Burt Boggess' store was all under water but the roof.

Then down Robinson's Run the back water was almost to the top of our little covered bridge. Some people rowed through it in boats and a high water mark could always be seen in it afterward. Some one in the boat cut a notch at the top of the water, but it rose about eight inches after that.

The road has been changed since, but the stone approaches can still be seen.

Mary Cambric (colored) and her mother—Sister Lora, Amanda Drummond and I went in to see this very old lady, we were just very small girls. She was so glad to see us. She also said: "I'se a hundred and gwine on eleben yeahs old." This was true. She lived to be 113. You can read this on her grave stone in the Lumberport cemetery.

Our First Train Ride

THE M. R. railroad was built shortly after the 1888 flood; care was taken to make its bed above the high flood line. Our first ride on it was the lengthy trip from Lumberport to Gypsy Grove to some sort of special gathering. The train was crowded to capacity; we had hardly become settled in the train till it was time to get out again.

Gypsy Grove was a beautiful spot, an amusement park built by the railroad company. It adjoined our beloved campmeeting ground. Its name was later changed to Cheswood Park for the great chestnut trees which provided the shade for the park and campmeeting ground.

Later it was all abandoned to become the mining town of Gypsy.

Many of the Prospect Valley families had "tents" at the campmeeting, namely: Ogdens, Duncans, Denhams, Bartletts, Chalfants, Crowls, etc.

Once when we were on our way with our big wagon loaded with supplies and mother and we little folks (we generally crossed the river at the mouth of Robinson's Run,) the water was very high. They should have gone to Shinnston that time. Caleb Crile was driving, the horses had to swim. The wagon nearly upset as a floating log barely scraped the back end of the wagon.

The last regular campmeeting was in 1893; not long afterward the buildings were torn down and each owner either took the materials home or sold it at the public sale. My father, Melville Bartlett, bought the walnut pulpit table and I have it in my house today. It has been pounded by many a celebrated preacher, both white and colored. I have seen it piled with money after the collection plates had been passed.

On one occasion there was a long procession going over that same rough road. We had crossed the river and were passing the construction gang who were building the railroad. A large empty powder can came rolling down into the road, frightening some of the horses. Mr. Joseph Hardesty had a spill, but no one hurt. Their wagon was broken, and the family had to divide up and ride with others. Their daughter Bertha, later Mrs. Chester Piggott, rode with us.

Grandfather Chalfant and my father built their tent together, making it twice the size of others. We had two large rooms up stairs and three down, besides a small entry way at the back. The beds and long table with benches on either side were built in. We never missed a session, and some times would stay for the colored campmeeting the following ten days, always in the month of August from Friday through to the second Sunday night. Then on Monday morning we would go home.

Playmates

THE D. Albert Hardesty family and ours were constant friends from babyhood till the present time, though circumstances have scattered us into many states of the Union. There were the same number of children in each family. We would take turns visiting each other, even the entire family would go. Sometimes on a Sunday morning here would come Hardesty's fringed top carriage, a beauty, hoving into sight coming up our road. What a scurrying of Lora, Charles, Howard and me and old Tray down to the big gate to open it for them, or more often they would come walking through the fields.

Then at another similar time, father would say: "Tenie, let's all go up to Albert's today," and away we would go.

Florence was nearer my age. She spent a great deal of time at my grandmother's with me. I was supposed to be there to help grandmother, but we did mostly playing.

Ada Flowers stayed there with me quite a lot also, sometimes both were there; grandmother was a patient soul. Once grandfather came home when we were all three there and he said, "Net, I've heard it said, 'One gal is a gal, two gals is a half a gal, and three gals is no gal at al'!" so Florence, you go home, now, till Ada gets her visit out then you can have your turn." And believe me, when he said "Scat," we always "scatted."

Nellie Wyatt was another good friend, but they lived there such a short while. They went to our school only one winter, then moved to Shinnston.

Once she and her brother, Russell, and I went to hunt raspberries, more for the picnicking than for berries, for we could have found plenty of berries right on our own farm. Their grandmother and my mother fixed us a lunch. We roamed those hills all day, starting with that Lucas mountain in front of our house, circling around toward Lumberport, keeping to the hilltops, thence to Joe Heldreth's farm, D. A. Hardesty's, stopped about there to eat lunch, then back through John Flowers' farm to our own, each having about a quart of berries; we went around our "little meadow" fence, that beautiful mound you can see from the church looking toward Clarksburg, there we filled our pails in a few minutes.

Nellie was a beautiful girl. She afterward married Robert Monroe, son of J. Walker Monroe, of Shinnston.

The church had no bell until Emma Ogden, Betty Robinson (Mrs. Col McCarty, daughter of James Robinson) and Lora Bartlett, who were then little girls, were appointed to get subscriptions. A prize was to be given to the one collecting the most. Lora was the winner, but the pious brethren, after receiving the money, said: "We decided we wouldn't give any prize." Lora gave her expression of disgust every time she thought of it the rest of her life.

Gypsies

NEAR the mouth of Robinson's Run was a favorite camping spot for gypsy caravans. It was a great thrill to visit them and have your fortune told. Once one of the fortune tellers told Amanda Drummond and me that if we would bring them a bucket of water, she would tell our fortunes.

We went across the river which was very low at the time, we hopped from stone to stone, and also waded some. She predicted us a great future, and we believed every word. We went to the old Denham house for the water. A family named Moore lived there.

One of the most condemned pleasures in those days was dancing.

If anyone gave a party and dared to so much as "Strip the Willow," they were disgraced for life in the eyes of the long-faced deacons, elders and scribes. His Satanic Majesty himself lived in the fiddle.

But it was perfectly proper to play post office and copenhagen. Those were the kissing games which were always played at the last day of school.

That day meant more to us than the present day commencement with its college degree and cap and gown.

There is still in existence a few copies of a photograph of the school when Burtice Ogden taught. The photo was taken on February 16, 1890. His name and date is on the back of our copy in the teacher's writing.

Those in the picture are:

Left to right, back row—(1) Lora Bartlett, (2) Emma Ogden, (3) Belle Drummond, (4) Marshall W. Ogden, (5) Homer A. Bartlett, (6) Burtice Ogden, teacher, (7) Jacob Harbert, (8) Ellsworth Ogden, (9) Russell Martin, (10) Henry Bartlett, (11) Alden Sprout, (12) Jim Lindsey, (13) Arthur Drummond.

PROSPECT VALLEY SCHOOL, FEBRUARY 16, 1890.

PROSPECT VALLEY SCHOOL, 1898

Second row—(14) Nettie Bartlett, (15) Martha (Toad) Moffatt, (16) Maggie Sprout, (17) Florida (Sis) Moffatt, (18) Malvina Lindsey, (19) Amanda Drummond, (20) Gertrude Morgan, (21) John N. Martin, (22) Wilmer Martin, (23) Allison (Jaky) Sprout, (24) Tom Lindsey (25) Will Lindsey, (26) Nathan Harbert (Nathan had a boil on his neck at the time).

Third row—(27) Howard Bartlett (not quite six years old, came especially that day to have his picture taken, (note his light blue bow and his big brother Charles' hand-me-down suit), (28) Lillian Morgan, (29) Margaret Harbert, (30) May Harbert, (31) Ernie Morgan and (32) Charles Bartlett.

Others not present that day are Jessie and Blanche Sturm, Ada Flowers, Charles Martin, Peyton Moffatt and probably others.

It includes the entire families (except Janie) of V. B. Ogden and M. B. Bartlett.

Note my made-to-measure shoes, made by V. B. Ogden. My dress is brilliant red with tiny white up and down stripes. I am also wearing a brooch that was purchased from the then famous J. Lynn and Co., 48 Bond St., New York.

A picture was taken at the new school in the winter of 1897-98.

We did not know the photographer was coming. It was a very bad, wintry day and several were absent. The county superintendent, Mr. Jas. E. Law, happened to make his visit that same day.

I had graduated the year before and was taking a post graduate course. Mr. Geo. Martin had taught school more than forty years.

First row—Leslie Ridge, Daisy Shreve, May Harbert, Allison Sprout, Ina Daugherty, Geo. Martin, teacher, Ada Flowers, Nettie Bartlett, County Superintendent Law, Lora Sprout.

Second row—Carl Martin, Remmie Shreve, Ernie Morgan, Christena Martin, Leota Harbert, Charles Flowers, Carrie Drummond, and Willie Flowers.

The upper school; the winter of 1895-96.

Left to right—Emma Hardesty, Erlen Hardesty, teacher, Martha Cunningham, Henry Robinson, Carl Robinson, Amos Robinson, Ed. Hardesty, Tally Haggerty, Chester Haggerty, Florence Hardesty, Elsie Hardesty, Nellie Robinson, Eva Robinson, Joe Haggerty, Anna Hardesty, Dessie Coffman, Lenna Haggerty, Lacie Robinson, Grace Haggerty, Lonnie McIntire, Robt. Taylor.

Evan Lanham, Hudson Robinson, Kenneth Robinson, Hannah Lanham, Willis Robinson, Glen Robinson, Edward Robinson, Clarence Amos, teacher, Ondas Lanham, Waymond Robinson, Vera Robinson, Enid Lanham, Audra Lanham.

About the year of 1889 or 1890 the school was divided. Then there was the "Upper" school and the "Lower" school. At first the Upper school was taught in the small house at the foot of the hill road near the Robinson homes; not long after (in the early 90's) we had new school houses. Ours was built right in Prospect. Even that has now been abandoned, as the children are taken in the school bus to Lumberport. Miss Nollie Taylor, of Clarksburg, was the first teacher in the new one.

It was a great event to visit our neighboring school on Friday afternoons, and to their last day of school, and there play the great game which was never played on any other occasion—copenhagen! In which we all stood in a circle, each holding our neighbor's hand, then one would be catcher, and would walk around the outside and "touch" some one who would run after him—or her—when caught they kissed, then the first one would stand in the ring and the other go around and choose.

UPPER SCHOOL, 1895-1896

UPPER SCHOOL, ABOUT 1910

There were always visitors from several schools on this occasion. From one of these there came two brothers, very nice chaps, too. They both were very freckled. Once when it was my turn to go around, I had just started when my little brother Charles, who was standing by looking on, yelled: "Net! Net!! touch one of them tuckey eggs!"

The Clarksburg Fair

IT WAS always a treat to get to go there. Sometimes we were fortunate to get to go two days, and just a few times we went three days.

That was before automobiles and it took two or three hours to get there. We always started before daylight; once we were almost the first ones through the gate.

One one occasion Albert Hardesty's and Lamar Robinson's families planned to go together. They lived on opposite hills and could see each others lighted windows. Hardestys arose and packed their lunch baskets, had breakfast, combed all those little red heads, dressed, and hitched up the horses——looking often across that great chasm to see any signs of life at Robinsons. Everything still was dark over there. They wanted to start before five A. M. They looked and looked, still no lighted windows. Then some one took a look at the clock——it was only about half past one. They very reluctantly undressed and went back to bed for a while.

The Tintype Man

MOST of those interested in these pages have at least one or two pictures in your family album that were taken in the tent that came in the summer and located beside the road near where it crosses Robinson's Run, right in Prospect. We have one in which is brother Homer, Arthur Drummond, Ben Burns and Marshall W. Ogden.

We also have some that were taken at the campmeeting ground, maybe by the same man.

Black Sam Wilson was the mail carrier before Matt Lindsey was appointed. He would also do white washing for people. When asked what he charged for his work he would always say: "Thutty cents a day." He was very small and short. He lived in Lumberport near Hornor's mill. He and his parents had belonged to the Stouts; the Otis Stout and E. K. Stout families.

Homer Bartlett recalls that in his boyhood, the swallows built nests under the eaves of the church its entire length. They would always come in droves in the springtime, then go away again in the fall.

Civil War Days
1861 to 1865

MANY of the boys whose names appear in these Sunday school class books were soldiers in this great conflict—and some never came back.

The farmers lost their best horses when the enemy sent scouts through to gather them up.

Mother's oldest sister, Minerva, made many a hurried trip with grandfather (John Chalfant). Each one riding one and leading as many as they could manage, they would flee to the wooded hills back from the road. Some times they would go to his other farm which was some where near the head of Jones' Run, a place that was then called Egypt. He never lost a horse.

Once when the report came that the scouts were coming through, Dr. Jesse Flowers, who was a Southern sympathizer rode proudly down to the road to greet them. They said: "That's a mighty fine hawse you're ridin', I guess we can use it."

"Oh, but I'm your friend," he said, "Well then you should be the more willing to help us, get off please." And he lost his fine horse.

Memories:
By Mrs. Elsie Flanagan

MY FIRST childish recollection of Prospect Valley church were in 1895. Most of the congregation came to church in sleds or on horseback, filling the pews to overflowing night after night during a revival.

Rev. Taylor Richmond is the first pastor I can remember.

The women of that day dressed quite differently from the modern fashions. I recall a head dress called a "fascinator" worn by many of the women. It resembled a hood with long, graceful streamers extending sometimes to the waist in the front; one I shall always remember— it had loops for bangs, was a deep pink in hue, and sparkling beads were interwoven in the loops.

The stone church's exterior was covered with a yellowish brown plaster, the interior was papered a pale green. From the center of the ceiling hung an immense brass chandelier of remarkable beauty. It held six oil lamps. These with two hanging lamps, having large white porcelain shades, suspended over the altar, and another lamp on the pulpit, provided ample light.

Across the entire front of the choir loft extended a white paneled alter. Two mourners' benches were on either side of the pulpit, and one directly in front. Never in later years have I seen any church furniture that seemed to me so beautiful. On the pulpit was a large Bible, bound in pig skin. The print was large and black and its pages were yellow with age.

The pews were the same ones that are now in use. They were painted in two shades of gray. Two burnside stoves heated the church. Beside each stove stood a coal hod, a three sided box shaped affair with one end open. The handle was an arched piece of hickory. I can well remember Mr. V. B. Ogden filling the stoves from these hods.

In a window to the right was a small bookcase, filled with spellers, primary readers, Bibles, etc. One book in particular, was peculiarly attractive to me. Its title I cannot recall, but it contained these lines:

> "The lark is up to meet the sun,
> The bee is on the wing.
> The ant its labor has begun,
> The woods with music ring."

The mode of travel was chiefly on horseback, and to accommodate these riders, were two upping blocks, one in the rear of the church and one to the front on the left. These were wooden platforms with two steps leading to the top.

My mother rode to church on horseback, carrying my younger sister in her lap, and with me and my older sister on behind. She rode side saddle and wore a long black riding skirt. But time has altered and hastened everything. The church of Prospect Valley will always be to me as it was in my childhood.

ELSIE HARDESTY FLANAGAN.

Mrs. Flanagan is the wife of Rev. Harry W. Flanagan, a minister in the Methodist Conference of West Virginia.

Prospect Valley History
August 10, 1937

STATEMENT by William Elmer Piggott, who was born on Piggott's Run, near Prospect Valley, on June 26, 1852, lived on Piggott's Run until 1871 and afterwards returned and taught school for one term in Harrison County at Henpeck or Respect or Margaret, and two terms at Pine Bluff:

I married Nancy Almeda Martin, daughter of Dorsey H. Martin. I am the oldest son of Milton Piggott who was born at either opposite Shinnston at the old Fortney farm or on Piggott's Run, but my earliest recollection was at Piggott's Run.

At the time of my earliest recollections, George Lucas lived on the hill near the mouth of Piggott's Run in a two-story log house. He and his brother, Basil Lucas, owned about all of the land on lower Robinson's Run between Shinnston, Lumberport and Prospect Valley. Basil Lucas was a bachelor and lived on the hill between Robinson's Run and Lumberport in a one and one-half story log house, afterwards owned by Luther Harbert and later occupied by Arthur Drummond. Lucas lived there with a colored man named Reason Childs and afterward moved in with his brother, George. In his old age he died in the George Lucas house, near the mouth of Piggott's Run.

Melville Bartlett's mother was a daughter of William Lucas, Sr., who was a brother to George and Basil Lucas. Basil never married. George Lucas' children were William, Jr., Edward, Rawley, Mary (Davis), Martha (Vincent), Amelia (Nixon), Amanda (Boggess). (See Lucas genealogy).

The next house up Robinson's Run was the Nathan Ogden house. He also operated a mill there when I was a boy, run by overshot waterpower, carried from a dam some distance up the run and a reserve dam at the present location of the Shinnston water dam.

Nathan Ogden was born across the river from Enterprise on the Leander Griffin farm and married Emily Duncan, who lived above Prospect Valley, near where Luther Piggott's house now stands. His brothers Samuel and Jonathan Ogden married sisters to Emily Duncan and they were sisters of Asbury Duncan, who was the father of John, Albert and Ezra.

Nathan Ogden continued to operate this mill until he died. Then his sons, Van B. Ogden, and Thomas Ogden and sister lived on the place for some years and operated the mill at intervals.

Dr. Jesse Flowers, who was a son of John Flowers, Sr., lived on the point between Piggott's Run and Robinson's Run, owned a farm there and practiced his profession from that point. His children were Dr. Basil Flowers, Dr. Caleb Flowers and a sister, Rachel, who married Dr. James Denham. Before Basil Flowers moved to the farm, he built a house on Piggott's Run, where Milton Piggott afterwards lived. He used the upstairs for a potting and pottery store, getting his clay from the neighborhood, and accumulated such a store of pottery people were afraid it might break in. He lived downstairs until well up in years, then moved over on the point between Robinson's Run, where he died

On the point by the Laurel Thicket lived John Flowers who taught a loud school there. The school was across the road from the house and was a one-story building about 20x30 feet, and the road ran from this house over to Piggott's Run.

A short distance west of this road and near the upper end of the present dam was a one and one-half story house in which Caleb Flowers lived. This was a little west of the old Indian fort erected in pioneer times.

I do not know who lived on top of the Abe hill.

(Abe Davis lived there for a time; the hill was named for him.—Ed.)

Mr. Elmer Piggott taught school for fifty-four years in Marion and Harrison counties. He gave some interesting talks in the Marion County McGuffey Society meetings during the years of 1936-37.

He also was much interested and a great help in getting material for this book.

His brothers, Ellis and Fletcher were good teachers also.

PIONEER DAYS

Before the days of many roads or the building of railroads, the farmers had to market their produce by means of flat boats, which were built in a boatyard at the mouth of Robinson's Run. Boats and cargo alike were sold in Pittsburgh and other down-the-river cities; then the men would have to walk back home. After 1852 they could come by railroad to Fairmont.

Rafts of logs were disposed of in the same way. John Chalfant drove a wagon and horses to Cumberland to get goods for his store and also brought "pig iron" to sell to blacksmiths. He would go to Baltimore by train from Cumberland, to get dry goods. Once he brought each of his daughters a lovely shawl. I still have my mother's. It is different from any usually seen; very long and narrow, to be looped up and draped over a hoop skirt costume.

John Flowers, who taught the loud school, was also a potter. His pottery was on Piggott's Run near the Milton Piggott home, now owned by Mr. Thos. Carrico. No doubt some of these old jars are still in the homes of this neighborhood.

THE INDIAN FORT

There was a block house or stockade for protection from the Indians located about a half mile below Prospect, about 500 feet back from the road and stream, in the field west of the present riding school, on what was later known as the Caleb Flowers place. For many years we could see a marked Indian grave in the laurel thicket, (now the site of the water reservoir).

Samuel Harbert, the ancestor of these Harbert families, had a fatal battle with Indians at Harbert's fort on Jones' Run. It is too harrowing to be written in these pages, but he can be found in other histories of this part of the state.

THE FIRST CHURCH ORGAN

Along in the late 1890's, the young people of the neighborhood began to realize the need of an organ in the church, and began investigations into the possibility of acquiring one. This resulted in consulting the catalogue of a well known mail order house, where we found that one could be had for $65.00.

It was decided that the best method of raising the money would be to have a water melon and ice cream festival on the lawn of the church; so several long tables were erected and covered with snowy linen, on which were placed many bouquets of flowers and sparkling oil lamps brought from our homes. Tall crystal cake stands held six- and seven-story cakes that would melt in your mouth. All this hemmed in by the border of locust trees, and the stone church in the background, made a pleasing scene. People came from far and wide. The melons were sliced unmercifully thin so they would serve a greater number of people, but no one seemed to mind. The ice cream was home made, from the richest of cream and new laid eggs eggs donated by the farmers.

The weather was ideal, the crowd remained till everything was sold out. Then when the treasurer's committee counted the money and yelled "sixty-five dollars and forty some cents," a rousing cheer echoed up and down that valley. In a very few days we had our organ and were proud, indeed, even though it was only a five octave reed organ. It wasn't many years till they got a better one, and now they have a good piano.

Each generation has had an enthusiastic group who have taken pride in keeping the church in good repair and have beautified it in many ways. The new windows have added much to its beauty.

PRANKS!

Marshall Ogden had a mania for playing pranks. His favorite sport was tying tin cans to dogs' tails. On one occasion, all the women of the neighborhood were having a quilting party at the home of Mrs. Ida Flowers. During the afternoon Marshall tied a can to "Ole Une," a hound belonging to Mrs. Sarah Cunningham (mother of Samuel Cunningham and Martha Dean). Of course the dog darted down the road to find her mistress, making a terrific noise; she never stopped till she reached Flowers' house, dashed through the house with a clatter, bang and howls; under the quilting frames to the feet of Sarah. Picture the scattering and shrieks of the ladies.

If there was a dead black snake menaceingly placed in the middle of the road, the frightened passerby would know it had been put there by "that Marshall!"

His sister, Janie, was as full of fun as he.

In later years Marshall Ogden became an able lawyer, was for many years the Prosecuting Attorney of Marion County. Practiced law with his son, Leland, in Fairmont, W. Va.

Extracts from Letters to the Shinnston News, Shinnston, W. Va.

By James Arthur Chalfant, Blackstone, Va.

JONES RAID IN 1863: My grandfather, Wm. Claiborne Denham, told me that after he heard these troops were coming up the river he went to his farm, just across from the month of Robinson's Run, to his brother's farm on the river, just below the old campmeeting grounds, and helped him (Dr. James Denham) hide his horses in the woods. They then went up to the top of the hill on Aaron Vincent's farm and were joined by the Vincents and others, watching for the army to come from Shinnston. Two scouts were in advance and my grandfather went down nearer the road and asked them what army was behind them. They said "Gen. Jones' army." He asked them which side they were on, they replied—"The right side, which side are you on?"

My grandfather jumped up, pointed his gun at them and said: "I am a Union man all through and all over." They dropped on the opposite side of their horses, and, coming up again, one lost his hold and fell to the ground. Grandfather did not let him remount, but captured the horse and raced up through the Vincent farm, and out into the woods where he hid the horse. The next day he delivered the horse and equipment to the Union Army headquarters at Clarksburg.

When some of these troops arrived at the home of Dr. James Denham they found my greataunt and her daughters putting out bedding, etc. She explained that they had just had a case of smallpox. For some reason these men went away at a full gallop, never stopping to look for horses, which they might have found in the woods.

There is an old graveyard on father's farm, just above the barn my father built in 1876. I've heard him speak of Sergeant Burns and other Burns buried there.

The first postmaster of Prospect Valley was Solomon H. Chalfant, who kept the postoffice in the store of his father, John Chalfant. (Solomon H. Chalfant gave it the name.)

This must have been prior to 1870. S. H. Chalfant resigned and recommended Van B. Ogden, who was appointed and moved the postoffice to his blacksmith shop just across Robinson's Run.

Mr. Ogden got a box in which boots were shipped to stores, and nailed it up on the wall of his shop, put a door and hinges, with a padlock on it, and this was the postoffice for many years. The box was wider at one end, as No 11 boots had been in one end and No. 5 boots in the other end.

Sarah Young came with the Adkinsons from Pocahontas County. The others went back finally, but Sarah married Greatuncle Daniel Mason, and she with her mother had a permanent home. Her mother outlived her but luckily for Uncle Daniel, she had a pension as a veteran's widow. Sarah was a great singer, and I can hear her yet singing "When the General Roll is Called Up Yonder, I'll Be There."

Mrs. Dudley Robinson told me that the Youngs were forced to flee from their home during the Civil War, and came to Prospect. You will find Sarah Young's name in the enclosed Sunday school record, both as pupil and teacher. "Grandma" Young smoked a pipe and also had a dog named Sailor, (N. B. C.)

Van B. Ogden and Benj. W. Harbert were boot and shoemakers, Mr. Ogden and Fred Nay were blacksmiths, also Joseph Baker, father of one-armed Mike Baker, who was constable and assessor.

The only lawyer I know of who can be credited to Prospect Valley is the Hon. Marshall W. Ogden, now residing in Fairmont. The only government clerk, I know of is the writer of this article, (J. A. C.)

The Economy bill of 1932 forced a bunch of us old timers to retire, and sit on the fence and watch the young fellows on their way to work.

Harvey W. Harmer's articles about the old mills are getting more and more interesting. I note that Wilson Sullivan was connected with the mill below the Shinnston bridge. His son, Elijah Sullivan, lived for some years at Peora, and dug wells in that vicinity. He dug a well for us. The first few feet was yellow clay and the last 38 feet was hard flint rock, which he blasted with black powder.

Mrs. Ellen Ogden, wife of Van B. Ogden, is listed as one of the Sunday school teachers in 1865. I remember of Van B. Ogden being the superintendent, also Asbury Duncan was class leader, as also was Luther Harbert, who was a Civil War veteran.

Albert Hardesty, father of Erlen B. Hardesty, was a classmate of mine in the public schools, though much older. He married Mary Michael. John Duncan married her sister, Susan.

Arthur Drummond was also one of my schoolmates.

EXTRACTS FROM CHALFANT LETTERS

Box 104, Blackstone, Va., May 29, 1937.

Editor News: Recently I received in the mail a history of Prospect Valley, prepared by Miss Bertha Coffman in 1925. This history does the writer credit, the arrangement is excellent. However, there is a little confusion under "schools." My father told me that he went to a school taught by John Flowers in his kitchen near the Laurel Thicket.

The thicket was on the site of the present water reservoir. The kitchen was the full length of a long house, and was wide enough to accommodate the pupils. My grandfather sent his children there for some years prior to 1855, when the old schoolhouse at the mouth of Harbert's branch of Robinson's Run burned. My grandfather then built a small school house near the old one. I remember distinctly of seeing it, and of seeing George Fletcher, who taught school in it before the public school house was built in 1867.

Peter Goodwin had taught school in it also. Neither of them ever taught in the new school house. The first winter I went to school was in 1870-71, B. Frank Martin was the teacher. He also taught the next winter. Afterward, Rawley Lucas, Seymour Piggott, Felix Martin, Dudley P. Moore, Moses S. Duncan and others taught there.

I remember when school elections were held, and votes were cast for and against school levy. If the majority voted for no levy, there would be no funds available, and of course, no school that year, but I think that never happened, although I knew some men who were outspoken against "free schools," and regularly voted for "no levy." Although the public or free schools have been in existence for seventy years, some people have failed to send their children, with the result that a compulsory school law was enacted.

My sister, Dr. E. Martha Chalfant, has a copy of an agreement made May 20, 1857, between Levi L. Kennett and Wm. Claiborne Denham, John Chalfant, and Asbury P. Sturm, a building committee of the Methodist church on Robinson's Run, at what is now Prospect Valley. This agreement covers the erection of a church building to be built of picked up stone, and to be 30 by 42 feet inside dimensions, exclusive of the walls. The walls to extend 20 inches under ground, and 14 feet from the upper surface of the ground. The floor to be one inch oak, jointed and five inches wide. The walls to be 21 inches thick, plastered in and out. To have nine (9) windows, three on each side, two in the pulpit end, and one in the other end between the two doors. The aisles were to be $3\frac{1}{2}$ feet wide each. The pulpit to be the same as the pulpit in the M. E. church at Barracksville. The roof the same as the church in Shinnston. The contractor, Levi L. Kennett, is to be allowed to pick up the stone on the lands of the committeemen. He is to furnish all other material, and to complete the job by December 25, 1858. He is to board himself and to be paid $935.00 for the completed church. On June 16, 1858, he acknowledged receipt of payment in full. It was specified that no bell was to be furnished and no place provided for one. About 1890, however, a bell was procured and installed. I remember when a small boy, that the women and children sat in the center of the church between the two aisles, while the men folks sat on each side next to the walls. A coal stove was provided on each side. The pulpit was raised so that two steps were necessary.

Three long flat altar seats were there. Also two long benches on each side in the "Amen Corner." A brass chandelier consisting of ornamental lamps, burning oil, hung in the center. Owing to leaks in the roof, the plastering, which must have been one inch thick, fell down in patches until most of it was gone, and they ceiled it overhead along in the eighties.—J. A. C.

Note: That beautiful snow white interior gave the impression of "Marble Halls." Those graceful curves in the wall at the windows added a distinctive touch. In the center of the ceiling and surrounding the chandelier, there was an artistically molded circle about four feet in diameter, that had the appearance of whirling. The chandelier must have been lacquered, because it was always brilliant and never tarnished. We could see our tiny reflection in it in a hundred places when sitting under it. It was taken out when gas light were installed. It is said to still be up in the loft. I hope it will be taken out and wired for electricity.

While building the church, Mr. Kennett lived in the long store building mentioned elsewhere, he had one son who was a very fat boy.

Above—Nettie Cooper, Basil Harbert and Homer Bartlett
Below—John Lucas

The local men volunteered their free services and teams to gather the stone. Mr. Kennett had also built the Barracksville church in 1854. It was smaller than ours, but has been enlarged since. Rev. Gordon Battelle dedicated both churches.

Read the story of the bell on another page.—Ed.

Blackstone, Va., June 21, 1937.

Dr. Jesse Flowers was the son of John Flowers, Sr., who lived across from the Laurel Thicket, and taught school in his long shed kitchen. My father has told me about going to school there, and that it was a "loud school." He said George Holder and Green Ogden were in one end where a ham was hanging, and were amusing the others by growling like tomcats around the ham, while Prof. Flowers was at the other end of the room, and couldn't hear a thing.

Dr. Jesse Flowers married Poppy Lucas, sister to George, Basil and William, Sr., and they had a daughter, Rachel, who married Dr. James Denham, father of Dr. Cecil Denham, who has been connected with the hospital at Weston. Dr. Basil Flowers, a son of Dr. Jesse, went west. I remember one of his daughters coming back on a visit. Another son, Dr. Caleb, lived, when I first remember him, just across from his grandfather, Prof. John Flowers, Sr. He afterwards lived next door to Van B. Ogden, and then where A. J. (Dolph) Shreve now lives. Then he moved to Sardis where he died.

His daughter, Viola, married Taylor Hess, and Elizabeth married Joshua Hess. One of Elizabeth's daughters married Edgar Harmer. Arthur and Newton Flowers became doctors in Clarksburg. John Flowers, Jr., bought Uncle Melville Bartlett out. Basil Lucas, bachelor, lived on the hill just above M. B. Bartlett.

On a branch of Piggott's Run, lived Joseph Exline, a class leader at Wesley Chapel. One time he and his family worked all day on Sunday, and came over the hills on Monday morning, and found Asbury Duncan and his boys hard at work. He said: "Why, Brother Duncan, what are you doing at work on Sunday?" Mr. Duncan convinced him of his mistake after a long argument.

Dr. Jacob Fortney owned a farm just over the hill from our old orchard, and his son, Rev. Granville (Bud) Fortney, now of Wyatt, lived there for some time. Joshua Fortney, brother of Dr. Jacob and father of Hiram, Seth, John O., and Naomi, the wife of Dr. Caleb Flowers, had a farm around in the next hollow toward Bingamon. Marion and John Shreve bought out the heirs of Joshua Fortney, then John bought out Marion, and part of Dr. Jacob Fortney's farm. Bisk Shreve now lives where John Shreve lived. Jacob Shreve, Sr., father of John, Marion, Noah, and others at one time lived above where Bisk now lives.

Milton Piggott lived just below, in the house of his father, Jesse, Sr. Just to the right of the old orchard lived John Duncan, Sr., father of Asbury and Dr. David Duncan. Back on the hill on the Asbury Duncan farm is a graveyard where some of them are buried. Dr. David Duncan built the house that my father and mother went to housekeeping in at the foot of the point below our home (Wm. Chalfant's). There was an old apple tree there the last time I was up, that my father said was there when he was a boy. I cut my name and date—1875—on a beech tree just over the point. It was there yet in 1919.

Jonathan Ogden lived just below where Luther Pigott built his house. He was a brother of Nathan Ogden, who had a flouring and grist mill run by overshot wheel down below the Shinnston water works. He also had a saw mill and shop. Used to make wooden bowls.

Rev. Asbury Sturm lived first at the mouth of the branch on which Benj. W. Harbert lived, and afterward on the corner below the old stone church.

At the head of this branch lived a United Brethren when I first remember, by the name of J. W. Boggess.

Down in the bottom lived William Moore, who owned a lot of land, and had two daughteres. One of them married a Heldreth (I think), and the other married Benj. W. Harbert.

There were several families above the Coffman place, Peyton and Lemuel Rogers, etc. I remember going to school with the Rogers and Coffman children. There were some Winemillers up at the head of the run. John Coffman bought them all out. Also down under our hill lived Peter Crim, Sr., and Peter Crim, Jr., Jefferson Crim, Calvin Drummond, Willie Drummond and others. Up the road above us lived Az. Drain, Henry Glaspell, etc. I have heard my father say that Peter Crim, Sr., was the first patient that Dr. Jesse Flowers had, and that Peter had a severe headache to which he was subject. Dr. Jesse did all he could for him, and went home, telling his wife that he heard Peter groaning until he got to the top of the hill and that if Peter died he would never take another case, but Peter got well and Dr. Jesse Flowers became famous.

He was called to see a man whose leg had been mashed at a house raising, and as there was no surgeon closer than Clarksburg or Morgantown, he had to get some man to sit on the patient and hold him down. (No anesthetics being available.) The doctor cut his leg off with a butcher knife and a handsaw, as I have heard from my father.

V. B. Ogden and Benj. W. Harbert built a storehouse in front of Mr. Ogden's house. It burned in 1876, then they built a brick storehouse below the road and kept store there a number of years. Afterward Charles Watkins kept store in it for Carder and Lowe of Shinnston.

A few words now about my grandfather, Wm. Claiborne Denham. He was a business man, besides farming on his large farm on the river just across from the mouth of Robinson's Run; he bought trees, hired men to cut them down, some were cut into logs, and many of them into what they called steam timber or steam sticks, (these were used for making steamboats), hewed flat on two sides, then rafted and run down the river for sale.

I have seen them starting off. Bert Drummond was always a pilot, and he would be at the rear end of the raft shouting "Lay her over there, boys." Grandfather Denham was also a good preacher. He gave a Bible and hymn book to Wesley Chapel when it was built.—J. A. C.

Miscellaneous Newspaper Clippings Collected by the Author

DO YOU remember Black Rease (or Rezin) slave of Basil Lucas? Rezin's family was separated by an act of the Virginia legislature. Basil Lucas was a bachelor living on his estate between Shinnston and Lumberport. Rezin was his faithful slave. West Virginia had not been separated from the mother state. The slave had a sweetheart, a Negro girl who was free, so after a time he decided to get married and the free girl became his wife. Several children were born to them and everything went well until Virginia passed a law prohibiting free Negroes from making their home in the state. This cruel act of the legislature made Rezin's wife an unlawful resident of the state. As the husband wanted to remain with his master it was finally decided that they separate. The wife took the children and fled to Pennsylvania, a free state. After a time two of the boys decided to make a visit to their daddy. It was necessary for them to make a secret trip, so they traveled on foot at night and hid out during the day. At Fairmont one of the boys was caught and sent back to Pennsylvania. The other lad made it through to the home of my grandmother, who hid him during the day and he went to see his father at night. Rezin outlived Basil Lucas but his master provided for his keep. Basil Lucas was a brother of George Lucas and an uncle of William, Edward, and R. G. Lucas

(Recalled by Elmer Piggott in the "Do You Remember Column" Fairmont Times.)

Rezin Childs later married Maria, who had belonged to Hornors. The Rezin's lived in the house that stood where the reservoir now is. He died there. Maria outlived him many years and was a real black mammy to the Bartlett children and also to Rawley Lucas' children.

Eagle District Teachers, 1896-7; Report by J. N. Stiles, President of Board of Education, Van B. Ogden; members, M. K. Baker, secretary, F. W. Cunningham.

Salary paid No. 1, $33.00; No. 2, $30.00; No. 3, $20.00. District No. 5, Prospect Valley school. Erlen B. Hardesty, the teacher. Trustees, M. B. Bartlett, A. J. Shreve, Wm. Chalfant. Graduates Alden Sprout, Allison Sprout, Nettie Bartlett.

District No. 16, Upper Robinson Run school. Essel M. Robinson, teacher. Trustees, Luther Coffman, Jas. A. Robinson, Lemar Robinson. Graduates, Carl W. Robinson, Leslie Haggerty, Henry C. Robinson, Edda Hardesty.

Prospect Valley. (Shinnston News May 20, 1898)

Florence Hardesty and Lora Bartlett were in Clarksburg Monday. Lloyd Chalfant was visiting at Weston last week.

Eddy Hardesty surprised us by calling on a girl in town Sunday evening.

Fletcher Piggott and Leslie Haggerty, who are attending school at Sardis, were visiting at their parents' homes the latter part of the week.

George and May Nixon were visiting Joe Lucas Sunday.

William Chalfant made a business trip to Fairmont Monday of this week. V. B. Ogden attended county court at Fairmont Wednesday.

Essel Robinson was the guest of Miss Blanche Sturm Sunday. Charley Bartlett and Arthur Drummond were at Clarksburg Wednesday.

Annie Hardesty was visiting at Bartlett's last week.
BUDA-PESTH.

An Air Mail Letter From Utah Jan. 30, 1930

No. 21 Hillcrest Apartments
Salt Lake City, Utah.

To the Shinnston News:

I must tell you how much I enjoy reading The News.

although a busy woman, I always take time to read "Our Paper."

I read of many people whose forebears of long, long ago were kinfolk with mine. Away back with the coming of the Mayflower, perhaps before.. My father talked so much of West Virginia, the early days, the Indians, their atrocious crimes; the wild animals.

These thrilling stories filled my childhood with awe. As I grew older father would speak of the Shinns,, (Ruth and Orpha), Harberts, Harveys, (my grandmother's people), Pigotts, Cunninghams, Boggesses, and others. These families have intermarried, thus uniting us as one big family.

In my genealogy research work I have written quite a number of letters to various parts of West Virginia and in return have received such gracious replies; many thanks to those good people for their kind assistance. I take this opportunity to extend greetings and pray the Lord to bless and prosper them through the New Year.

A relative from Utah,

MRS. FLORA HARVEY SUNDBERG.

July 1937. M. W. Ogden, of Fairmont, was chosen president of the Prospect Valley Homecoming Association at its annual meeting Sunday.

E. B. Hardesty was named vice president and Mrs. Nettie Bartlett Cooper, of Fairmont, secretary.

Talks on Robinson's Run history were given by Harvey W. Harmer and W. Guy Tetrick, of Clarksburg.

Mr. and Mrs. Hardesty Entertain

Mr. and Mrs. James L. Hardesty entertained a number of relatives at their home near Wyatt Wednesday afternoon, July 14, in celebration of the 56th wedding anniversary. The home was a vision of loveliness, with beautiful flowers gathered from the gardens, artistically arranged on tables and mantle pieces.

During the afternoon refreshments were served. Those present were: Mr. and Mrs. R. R. Hardesty, Mrs. E. L. Piggott, Mr. and Mrs. G. A. Hardesty, Mrs. J. H. McGee, Miss Adah McGee, Mrs. John H. Musgrave, Mrs. D. J. Carter, Mr. and Mrs. L. S. McGee, Betty and Martha McGee, Mr. and Mrs. J. Seyward Hardesty, Genevieve, Doris and James Hardesty, all of Shinnston and Prospect; Mr. and Mrs. G. W. Cunningham and Homer Bartlett, of Clarksburg.

Shinnston News, May, 1938:—Virginia had no free schools in 1863. John Chalfant, of Robinson's Run, was a great believer in education. He built a frame school house on his land, and employed a good teacher from Pennsylvania. His name was George Fletcher. It was my first school and he was my hero. I decided I would be a school teacher. I recall these scholars: Charles W. Lynch, who became Judge Lynch, George Lucas, Rawley Lucas, Melville Bartlett, Mar Patterson, Sol, Minerva, and Christena Chalfant, Jane and Verna Sturm. Some of the younger ones were Thomas Flowers, Ben and Frances Flowers, my brother and I. Mr. Fletcher taught McGuffey's readers, Pinneo's grammar, Ray's arithmetic, Frey's geography, and spelling.

ELMORE PIGGOTT.

Guest From Cincinnati

Miss Marguerite Rowan, of Cincinnati was a recent guest of friends here. She came here from Grafton, where she visited her uncle and aunt, the Rev. and Mrs. Harry W. Flanagan. Miss Rowan, who has been blind since childhood, is a linotype operator, and is located at Clovernook, a home for blind women near Cincinnati. This home was formerly the homestead of the poets, Alice and Phoebe Carey. Miss Rowan occupies the room once used by the Misses Carey, and uses some of the furniture once owned by the sister poets. She is the daughter of the late Edward and Emma (Hardesty) Rowan.

April 1938:—Mrs. Nettie Bartlett Cooper will have on exhibition at the Women's Clubs art exhibit at Clarksburg, April 18 to 23, her recently completed painting of the old Levi Shinn log house on Mrs. C. S. Randall's farm, south of Shinnston.

This house is said to be older than the Constitution of the United States. She will also have two or three more of her paintings on display. Mrs. Cooper is now writing a history of the Prospect Valley community.

DEED FOR WESLEY CHAPEL CHURCH LOT

Harrison County Records. Deed Book No. 42, page 415.
    A. P. Sturm and Wife; Deed 116 Square Poles to
    M. E. Church Trustees.

This deed made this 14th day of July A. D., 1857, between Aspberry P. Sturm and Mary Ann, his wife, of Harrison County, Virginia, of the one part, and Jacob Bowman, James Denham, Aspberry P. Sturm, John Chalfant, William C. Denham, David Holder and F. M. Sturm, of the same place, trustees in trust for the uses and purposes hereinafter mentioned of the other part. Witnesseth, That the said Aspberry P. Sturm and Mary Ann, his wife, in consideration of Fifty Dollars, do grant unto the said Jacob Denham, James Denham, Aspberry P. Sturm, John Chalfant, W. C. Denham, David Holder and F. M. Sturm and their successors, trustees in trust for the uses and purposes hereinafter mentioned and declared, all a certain lot of or piece of land in the county and state aforesaid, on Robinson's Run, adjoining a lot of F. M. Sturm, and bounded as follows.: Beginning at a stake corner of F. M. Sturm, thence by a line of his S. $19\frac{3}{4}°$ W. 15 poles to main road, thence up same N. 75° W. 8 poles and 18 links to a stake in same, thence leaving road N. $15\frac{1}{2}°$ E. 14 poles to a stake, thence S. 82° and 20 minutes E. 7 poles, 17 links to the beginning, containing about 116 square poles. To have and to hold the above described lot of land to them, the said Jacob Bowman, James Denham, Aspberry P. Sturm, John Chalfant, William C. Denham, David Holder and F. M. Sturm and their successors in office forever, and the said Aspberry P. Sturm and Mary Ann, his wife, here coverants to a warrant "generally" the property hereby conveyed to the said trustees and their successors in office.

In trust, that they shall erect and build or cause to be erected or built thereon, a house or place of worship for the use of the members of the Methodist Episcopal Church in the United States of America, according to the rules and discipline which from time to time may be agreed upon and adopted by the ministers and preachers of the said church at their General Conference in the United States of America, and in further trust and confidence that they shall at all times forever hereafter permit such ministers and preachers belonging to the said church as shall from time to time be duly authorized by the General Conference of the ministers and preachers of the said Methodist Episcopal Church, or by their annual conference authorized by the said General Conference to preach and expound God's Holy Word therein; and in further trust and confidence that as often as any one or more of the trustees hereinbefore mentioned shall die or cease to be a member or members of the said church according to the rules and discipline as aforesaid, then and on such cases it shall be the duty of the stationed minister or preacher (authorized as aforesaid) who shall have the pastorial charge of the members of the said church, to call a meeting of the remaining trustees as soon as may conveniently be, and when so met the said minister or preacher shall proceed to nominate one more person to fill the place or places of him or them whose office or offices has or have been vacated as aforesaid, provided the person or persons so nominated shall have been one year a member or members of said church immediately preceding such nomination, and shall be at least 21 years of age, and the said trustees assembled shall proceed to elect and by a majority of votes appoint the person or persons so nominated to fill such vacancy or vacancies in order to keep up the members of seven trustees forever, and in case of an equal number of votes for and against the said nomination the stated minister or preacher shall have the casting vote, and the said Aspberry P. Sturm and Mary Ann, his wife, do covenant as aforesaid to warrant generally the property hereby conveyed to the said Jacob Bowman, John Denham, Aspberry P. Sturm, John Chalfant, William C. Denham, David Holder and F. M. Sturm and their successors chosen or appointed as aforesaid.

In Testimony that of the said Aspberry P. Sturm and Mary Ann, his wife, have hereunto subscribed their names and affixed their seals on the date above written.

MARY ANN STURM,, (Seal)

Grantors

A. P. STURM, (Seal)

By the term Methodist Episcopal Church in the foregoing deed is meant only that portion of Methodists sometimes distinguished as the Methodist Episcopal Church North.

Wesley Chapel Methodist Episcopal Church, Lumberport Circuit, Sept. 10, 1925——

R. G. LUCAS,
ANNIE HARDESTY MARTIN,
EMMA ROBINSON,
JESSIE COFFMAN,
CARL W. ROBINSON,
BERTHA COFFMAN,

Trustees.

EXTRACTS FROM SUNDAY SCHOOL RECORDS FROM 1894 TO 1897

May 20, 1894—Number present 70. Rev. Taylor Richmond being with us, he took charge of Class No. 1.

May 27—Sunday school called to order by Assistant Superintendent D. Albert Hardesty. Number present, 65.

June 17—Prayer led by Rev. A. P. Sturm. Number present, 100.

July 15—Superintendent R. G. Lucas, number present, 37, six verses from the Book of Jeremiah were delivered from memory by Miss May Harbert. C. Belle Drummond, secretary.

August 12—A. A. Haggerty gave a fine talk on the subject of Sunday school. Number present, 28. Emma D. Hardesty, secretary pro tem.

September 30—Election of officers for coming quarter, superintendent, Ellsworth Ogden; assistant superintendent, Mrs. Albert Hardesty; secretary, Miss Jessie Sturm; treasurer, Nettie Bartlett; librarian, Ina Daugherty. Teachers: Class No. 1, R. G. Lucas; No. 2, Arthur Drummond; No. 3, M. W. Ogden; No. 4, M. B. Bartlett.

December 30—Sunday school met at 2 P. M. Prayer by E. E. Ogden Number present, 64. Review lesson proved unusually interesting and school was prolonged until a late hour. Then adjourned to make way for preaching by Rev. Taylor Richmond.

January 13, 1895—The weather being very bad, many scholars were absent. Number present, 24.

February 10—All teachers present. Number scholars, 55. School led in prayer by Mrs. Mary Lucas.

March 31—Quarterly election of officers, E. E. Ogden, resigning. Superintendent, R. G. Lucas; assistant superintendent, Mrs. Rosa Coffman; secretary, Lora Bartlett; treasurer, Ellis Piggott. Teachers: Class No. 1, Mrs. Rosa Coffman; No. 2, E. E. Ogden; No. 3, Jessie Sturm; No. 4, Mrs. Lily Ogden.

January 5, 1896—Secretary, Amanda Drummond; librarian, Ada Flowers.

November 22, 1896—Teachers: No. 1, A. P. Sturm;

SUNDAY SCHOOL IN 1909

No. 2, E. E. Ogden; No. 3, Fred McIntire; No. 4, Mrs. Lyda Sturm; treasurer Florence Hardesty.

June 19, 1897—Plans were made for Children's Day.

THE PROSPECT VALLEY COMMUNITY CLUB

This Club was organized in 1922 for the purpose of bettering the social, educational and spiritual life of the community. Twelve committees are appointed each year to raise the standard of their particular part of the community life, and also to give a program in the month most suitable. The different divisions stress the fact that the essentials for a well balanced community life are churches, schools, homes, health, recreation, farms, business, community spirit and good citizenship. This organization has been a great help to the community.

Later in the same year of 1922, women of the community got together and organized a club which they named the Woman's Welfare Club, with twelve charter members. Four of these members have since passed away, but others have joined and at the presnt time the club has twenty-three members, living not only in the immediate community, but also in Shinnston and Lumberport. This club does very much the same work as a ladies' aid, and in the past sixteen years has spent several hundred dollars for the church and other worthwhile things. The latest project is buying the old Prospect Valley school house, to be used as a recreation center. This school house was built about 1892, and was used till the bus system was established for carrying the scholars to Lumberport schools.—(1938)

The "Upper school" house was located on the road between the farms of James and Lamar Robinson, and has since been remodeled for a dwelling.

Around the 1920's the McGinnis family lived at the mouth of Pigott's Run, and were an important factor in the church and Sunday school. Mrs. McGinnis was so capable in all community activities. They were sorely missed when they went away. The children's names were John, Marian, Mary, Nelle, Gene, David, and Archie.

PROSPECT VALLEY SUNDAY SCHOOL REGISTER IN 1937-38

Superintendent—Mrs. Dessie Richardson. Assistant superintendent, Mrs. Jessie Hardesty; secretary, Miss Rhoda Robinson; treasurer, Mr. Dale Nay.

Class No. 1—Teacher, Miss Virginia Lee Robinson.

Charles Nay
Paul Gessler
Loretta Gessler
Doris Gene Hall
Charles Robinson
Gene Martin
Betty Ray Robinson
Willard Harbert
Josephine Piggott
Harold Scott
Dicky Kester
—— Kester

Class No. 2—Teacher, Mrs. Jessie C. Hardesty.

Betty Moore
Pauline Gross
Maxine Piggott
June Robinson
Katherine Ashcraft
Hayward Harbert

Class No. 3—Teacher, Miss Bertha Coffman.

Elizabeth Coffman
Ellen Robinson
Jean Nay
Eva Scott
Junior Moore
Danny Moss
Robert Tichenor
Paul Fortney
Lillian Fortney
Doris Jean Kester
Kenneth Ashcraft
James Hardesty

Class No. 4—Teacher, Mrs. Dessie C. Richardson.

Geraldine Scott
Mildred Davis
Marjorie Ann Robinson
Emma Mae Tichenor
Anna Lorna Robinson
George Lee Martin
Marcella Robinson
Darrell Robinson
Junior Piggott
Junior Davis
Everett Scott
Elsie McKneely
Brooks Kester

Class No. 5—Teacher, Mr. Dale Nay.

Gene Richardson
Genevieve Hardesty
Pauline Pierson
Doris Hardesty
June Martin

Margaret Martin
Junior Robinson
Warren Ashcraft
Mabel Kester

Class No. 6—Teacher, Mr. Edwin B. Richardson.

L. W. Martin
Amos Robinson
Rosa Coffman
Flo Martin
Irene Ashcraft
Orha Hall
Edward Robinson
Alma Robinson
James T. Moss
Mrs. Rosella Moss
Mrs. Opal Moore
Dr. Martha Chalfant

Thos. Carrico
Mrs. Edith Nay
Erlen B. Hardesty
Mrs. Jennie Cunningham
Cora Martin
Mrs. Stella Kester
Arthur Scott
Herman Kester
Evelyn Harbert
Stella Coffman
Mrs. Willa Robinson
Delano Martin

Ashcraft Genealogy

THE first Ashcraft of which any definite information has been obtained for this chronicle, is John Ashcraft, who was a native of Fayette County, Pa.

He and four of his sons did service in the Revolutionary War—Amos, Uriah, John II, and Ezekiel.

Pennsylvania archives of the Revolutionary War show that Edward, John, Uriah, Levi, Amos, and James were in military service.

John Ashcraft, the father of the four above named, enlisted in 1781 in a Fayette county, Pa., company; marched to Fort Pitt, joined Gen. George Rogers Clarke's expedition to Wheeling, and was under Capt. Jacob Cline, serving six months in the regular army of the Revolutionary War. Later served one year under Sergeant Manuel Brown, and later went out on alarms against Indians. He applied for and received a pension July 28, 1832, aged 95 years.

He owned lands along the West Fork river in Harrison county, West Virginia. His son, Ezekiel, was too young to be a soldier, but his name appears on Capt. Nathaniel Cochran's muster roll as a drummer boy. The original papers are now possessed by Capt. Cochran's great grandson, Thomas M. Leeper, of Monongah, W. Va.

Ezekiel's descendants are the only line of which I will write here, as they belong to the community. The history of the others may be found in Wither's "Border Warfare" and Mr. Guy Tetrick's "Families of Northern West Virginia." Also in the Clarksburg Sunday Exponent Telegram, March 11, 1934. Records differ as to the date of Ezekiel's birth, but the Harrison county records show that he married April 21, 1823, Jane Nay, daughter of William Nay.

John and Uriah Ashcraft were Revolutionary soldiers and may have been brothers. Uriah Ashcraft married

September 6, 1772, Sarah McIntire, daughter of Elimiderson McIntire, (see "Marriage Bonds" in Harrison county court house). Uriah's second wife, Sarah Davis, married 1789.

The first Ezekiel Ashcraft married April 21, 1822, Jennie Nay, their son "Little Zeke," born in Harrison county, died in the Civil War, married Ellen Drain, born 1838, daughter of Axariah and Rosana (Collins) Drain. Ellen's second husband was Albert Pitcher.

Children of Ezekiel and Jennie Nay Ashcraft

"Little Ezekiel," Polly, Azariah, Arm, Caleb, Harris, Nancy (Mrs. Jim Burns), Rachel, (Mrs. David Minnix), Zachariah. (See Burns.)

Children of "Little Zeke" and Ellen Ashcraft.
Married February 17, 1853

1. Mary Jane, born 1853, died November 17, 1919, married Richard O. Martin. (See Martin.)
2. John, married Martha Miller. Children, Lily, Curt, Amanda, Ernest.
3. Louisa died December 14, 1929, married Arthur A. Haggerty. (See Haggerty.)
4. Geo. W., died August 14, 1899, married Alice Harvey.
5. Francis, born February 23, 1862, married 1884, Malvina Miller, born September 13, 1865.

Children of Francis and Malvina Miller Ashcraft

1. Rosella, born December 12, 1885; married December 4, 1904, Allison Sprout. 2. J. T. Moss.
2. Cora, born May 12, 1887, married July 4, 1904, Newton Fluharty.
3. Bessie, born October 5, 1889, married October 23, 1915, Arthur Martin.
4. Dessie, born October 5, 1889, married March 26, 1913, Joseph Fluharty.

5. Carrie J., born May 18, 1891, married June 6, 1910, Sanford Waginer, died May 14, 1920.

6. Howard, born August 30, 1894, married November 22, 1919, Edna French.

7. Emma, born September 2, 1897, married April 6, 1920, John King.

8. Estie Delaine, born June 25, 1905, married November 13, 1922, Robert Tichnell, died January 25, 1927.

Children of John and Martha (Miller) Ashcraft

Lily married Lloyd Haggerty. Amanda married Basil Crim. Curtis, Ernest. William married Lutie Stark. Curtis married Ola Boggess.

Burns Family

James Burns married Nancy Ashcraft, daughter Ezekiel and Jane N. Ashcraft, born 1820.

Children

Fred B., 1841, married Martha Cavilier. Went west.

John (Jack), born 1845, married ——White

Sarah, born 1846, married Benj. Cunningham, blind.

Louisa, born 1848, married Isaac Sprout, son of Wm. Sprout. (See Drummond.)

Mary (Lottie), married "Dock" Lindsay.

Columbia, married Fred McIntire. Children, Lonnie, Armatha, John A. P., Mabel.

Benj., married first, Martha Coffman; second, Rowena Davis.

One Thos. Burns is listed as a Revolutionary soldier in Capt. John Lewis' company, Botetourt county, Va. regiment.

Children of Benj. and Sarah (Burns) Cunningham. Samuel, Martha and Mary, born March 21, 1879, twins.

Martha, married Wesley Dean. Two daughters, Beatrice and Marie.

Mary, married Wilmer Martin, son of Richard O. M.

One daughter, Merle, married Glyde Robinson, son of Ransler Robinson.

Samuel, married first, Dickie Drain Ashcraft; second, Jennie Miracle. Children, Blanche, Dalphin.

Fred and Jefferson McIntire were sons of Nicholas McIntire.

Lonnie McIntire married Lucy Miller. Their children, 1 Walter, 2 Audrey, 3 Josephine, 4 Irene, 5 Orville.

ASHCRAFT AND BURNS GENEALOGY

Children of Dock and Mary Lottie (Burns) Lindsey

Ida, married ——Trecize.

Jim, married a daughter of Theodore Coffman.

Thomas, Claude, Malvina, Celia. Malvina married Thomas Ashcraft.

Children of Thomas and Malvina (Lindsey) Ashcraft

1, Ray; 2, Wayne, married Irene Carrico. 3, Mabel, 4, Madge.

ASHCRAFT AND HAGGERTY GENEALOGY

Children of Arthur and Louise (Ashcraft) Haggerty

1. Lloyd, married first, Jennie Moore; second, Lily Ashcraft, daughter John and Amanda A.
2. Leslie, married Nora Morrison. Children, Louise, Christine, Leslie, Jr.
3. Talbot, married Lora Sprout, daughter of Isaac Sprout.
4. Chester, married Rose Gaines. 5, Grace, married Frank Stout. 6, Lenna, married Comer Collins. 7, Joe. Amos, Pearl, married ——— Carper.

Ezekiel Ashcraft operated a cane mill for years and ground the cane for every farmer who raised it. A "stirring off" party was a great event.

John Burns or Byrns, married Ester Cavilier. He was sergeant in the Revolutionary War. They are buried on the William Chalfant farm on the hill between Prospect Valley and Peora. Their son, James Burns married December 20, 1844, Nancy Ashcraft in Harrison county. James had a brother, Isaac.

BARTLETT GENEALOGY

James Bartlett, Sr., does not appear in the Harrison county records as early as the other Bartletts.

He purchased land here in 1797 from Pierce and Mary Bailey, of Loudon county, Virginia. He married August 12, 1790, in Loudon county, Virginia, Sarah Phillips, daughter of Thomas and Mary (John) Phillips. (Mary John, daughter of William and Mary John whose wills on record in Loudon county, Virginia, mention daughter Mary Phillips). Thomas Phillips came to Harrison county and settled in that part included in Barbour county. His will recorded in Harrison county in 1798 mentions his wife, Mary, and two daughters: Sarah, wife of James Bartlett, and Catherine, wife of John Reynolds, and left bequests to his young grandsons, Robert Bartlett and Thomas Reynolds.

James Bartlett left no will and the following children are found through the death records:

1. Robert, born about 1791, died 1878, married Hannah Wamsley 1814. (Hannah W., daughter David Wamsley, Revolutionary soldier. See Wamsley genealogy.)

2. Matilda, born 1801, died 1867, married first Granville Stealey; second, Wm. Bartlett, 1825, son of John.

3. James P., born 1804, died 1872, married Cynthia Bartlett, daughter of Benjamin.

James P. Bartlett was proprietor of the old Bartlett hotel, prominent in the early history of Clarksburg.

4. Harriet, died 1874, married George Criss.

Robert Bartlett, born June 26, 1791, son of James and Sarah (Phillips) Bartlett; married March 16, 1814.

Hannah Wamsley, born June 29, 1789, daughter of David Wamsley of Big Elm farm. They are buried at Hepzibah, W. Va. (See Wamsley genealogy.)

Their son, Absalom, born January 12, 1819, died August 12, 1851. Buried at Sycamore Dale. Married November 17, 1842. (By Rev. Levi Shinn.)

Elizabeth Lucas, born September 1, 1824, died October 24, 1864. Buried in Lucas cemetery. Daughter of Wm. and Unity (Shinn) Lucas. (See Lucas genealogy.)

Absalom's son, Melville Basil Bartlett, born September 19, 1843, died July 8, 1920. Married November 11, 1869, by Rev. L. F. Benedum.

Christent Chalfant, born October 26, 1845, died August 13, 1936. Buried at Shinnston. (See Chalfant genealogy.)

Their children, all born at Prospect Valley, W. Va.

Homer Absalom Bartlett, born October 10, 1870. In State Legislature four years.

Solomon Henry, born November 10, 1871, died January 10, 1907. Buried at Columbus, Ohio. Married 1902 to Anna Powell of Columbus, Ohio.

Lora Alice, born March 6, 1876, died October 29, 1908.

Nettie M., born March 14, 1879, married Stanley Cooper of Cincinnati, Ohio, July 6, 1910.

Charles Leslie, born April 28, 1882, married 1927, Maude Woods, Detroit, Mich.

Charles children—James Erwin Bartlett, born July 13, 1928. Charles Leslie, Jr., born November 25, 1929.

Howard Robert, married Roberta Tandy, Phoenix, Arizona.

COPY OF WILL OF JOHN CHALFANT

Of Birmingham, Chester County, Pa., August 12, 1725

Be it remembered that I, John Chalfant, Gent., of Birmingham in the County of Chester, in the province of Pennsylvania, yeoman, being sick and weak of body, but of sound and perfect Mind and Memory, thanks be given to Almighty God for the same, and calling to mind the Mortality of this Mortal life—do make this my last will and Testament and as to the disposing of such Estate as it has pleased God to bless me withall to be disposed of in manner and form following:—I will that all my debts be paid and my funeral charges by my executor hereafter named. 2ndly item: I give and bequeath to my loving wife all my Estate, both real and personal during her natural life for her sustaining and Maintenance—but not to sell, give or waste.

Thirdly: My will is that what remains of my Estate after the death of my wife, be equally divided between my sons Robert and John, and further my will is that Ye part that falls to my son John Chalfant be put out to interest by my Executors hereafter named and they of ye survivor of them, to pay the Interest of the said half part during his life and after his death to be equally divided between his three eldest sons, Viz: John (3rd), Solomon and Robert. Lastly I do ordain, Constitute and make as my true and lawful Executors my son, Robert Chalfant, and John Beckingham, of Township of Birmingham, to whom I give full power and authority to sell my land and to convey the same as I myself might or could do. In testimony whereof I have hereunto set my hand and seal this twelfth day of August, Anno Domo, 1725. JOHN CHALFANT.

    Wits.   Mary Stevents
               Edward 1 1 1 Purtridge
  Proven August 25, 1725.
    (Bk. A. Page 172, Chester County Wills)

John (3) in the above will was the father of Solomon Chalfant, the Revolutionary soldier. John (1) was born in England. His sons, John (2) and Robert (1) born in Pennsylvania. Also John (2's) three sons.

Solomon, son of John (3), married Jemima Eaton. She was killed by Indians near their home at what is now Berkeley Springs, W. Va. She was out on the hillside gathering apples or berries, when a band of Indians shot her. Solomon and Jemima had one son, Robert (3), and several daughters. That son, Robert, is the ancestor of all the Chanfants in this community. He married Margaret Henkins. Their only son, John (4) born December 18, 1813, died May 7, 1908, married April 7, 1836, by Rev. Jeremiah Phillips, Phoebe Conaway, born October 24, 1815, died October 27, 1894, at Prospect Valley, W. Va. She was the daughter of Jeremiah and Mary (Brown) Conaway of Basnettsville, W. Va.

CHALFANT GENEALOGY

Chalfant St. Giles, Buckinghamshire, England, is the ancestral home of the Chalfants, and the name is of local origin.

The family of Chalfants is found there in the sixteenth century. John Chalfant is the first of the name in America about whom we have any information. John Chalfant came with William Penn in the good ship "Welcome" about 1683. He was granted a large tract of land in Chester county, Pa., and about 1699 he patented a tract of 250 acres in Rockland Manor, Chester county. He died in 1725 leaving two sons, (see will). We are descended from John (2nd). He had three sons, John (3rd), Robert (2nd), and Solomon (1). John Chalfant (3rd) had one son, Solomon (2).

Solomon (2), born January 25, 1753, died February 26, 1837, married Jemima Eaton.

They lived near what is now Berkeley Springs, W. Va. He was a Revolutionary soldier. They had one son, Robert (3), and several daughters.

1. Robert, born 1791 in Va., married Margaret Henkins

John (4), son of Robert and Margaret (Henkins) Chalfant, born December 18, 1813, died May 8, 1908, married April 4, 1836, by Rev. Jeremiah Phillips, Phoebe Conaway, daughter of Jeremiah and Mary Brown Conaway. She was born October 24, 1815, died October 27, 1894.

Children of John and Phoebe (Conaway) Chalfant

1. William, born May 8, 1837, died, August 30, 1921, buried at Oakdale.

2. Minerva, born July 27, 1839, died May, 1869. (See Lucas genealogy.)

3. Rebecca, died young (burned). Buried in Harbert Run cemetery.

4. Solomon, born, December 30, 1843, died, —— 1895. Buried at Shinnston.

5. Christena, born, October 26, 1845, died, Auust 13, 1936. (See Bartlett genealogy.)

6. Robert, born, June 27, 1847, died, December 15, 1911.

7. Mary, born June 2, 1849, died January 15. (See Lucas Genealogy.)

8. Jeremiah, born July 30, 1850, died, July 13, 1932, at East Liverpool, Ohio.

John, born, May 2, 1860 (at age 12, he weighed 185 lbs.) died March 3, 1873.

Wm. Chalfant, married March 6, 1861, Mary Denham, born July 6, 1841. (See Mason genealogy.) Their children:

1. James Arthur, born February 24, 1862, married July 4, 1892, Minnie D. Rose. She was a descendant of Alexander Hamilton. Have one daughter, Carrie Hazel Whyte.

2. Robert Russell, born, March 27, 1864, married, October 19, 1891, Elsie Stoneking; had children: Clarence, Homer Curtis, Flossie, Bessie and Ruby.

3. Claiborne Ellis, born, April 10, 1867, married, June 19, 1892, Gertrude Clark. His children: Mabel, Cletus, Mary, Nellie, Harvey, Lloyd W., Elizabeth and Anna.

4. Doctor Martha Estelle.

5. May, married October 19, 1803, Otto Reed, had two sons, Ward and Glenn. Ward married. Ward's

children: Margery, Jeanne, Earl. Glenn married Louise Boord.

6. Anna, born May 20, 1876, married, May 10. 1905, Rufus Ogden, son of Kidwell Ogden.

7. Lloyd, born, November 14, 1878, married, June 17, 1903, Willa Hoff. Lloyd's children, Guy, Helen and Fred. Helen married Easter Sunday, 1938, Earl Stansberry, Columbus, Ohio. One daughter, Jane Ellen Stansberry, born January 24, 1939.

Solomon Chalfant, married Margaret McCoy, 1893. One son, Clarence O.

Clarence O. Chalfant married Lucille Blaney. They live in West Alexander, Pa., and have two daughters.

1. Joan.
2. Mary Martha.

Minerva Chalfant married Edward Lucas. Their son Charles Fletcher Lucas married Marie Fowler. Their children: William married —— Cole; 2, Van Buren. William has one daughter, Barbara.

Jeremiah Chalfant married Nettie Slocum March 13, 1879. Their children, Orville, Ola, Blanche, and William.

Mary Chalfant married Rawley G. Lucas.

Children of Rawley and Mary Chalfant Lucas

John Renicks Lucas married Etta Willis.

Joseph G. Lucas married Tillie Richards. Aileen, Mary Jo.

Basil H. Lucas married Mayme Hardesty. One son, Basil, Jr.

For Christena Chalfant, (See Bartlett Genealogy.)

Children of Jeremiah and Nettie Slocum Chalfant

Iola Chalfant, married Dennis Jaynes.
Orville Chalfant, married Alice Patton.

Blanche Chalfant, married Lester Parsons, ———Parsons and ....Wamsley, parents.

William Chalfant, married Blanche Bice.

Children of Dennis and Iola C. Jaynes.

Mildred married Dale Messenger. One son, Jackie Dale Messenger.

Ethel married Dale McLaughlin.

Children of Orville and Alice Patton Chalfant

Marie and Martha.

Children of Lester and Blanche C. Parsons.

Donald and Louise.

Children of Wm. B. and Blanche Bice Chalfant.

Raymond, Catherine, and Wm. Burle, Jr.

COFFMAN GENEALOGY

The Coffmans are of German descent. The first of which we have record in America is Jacob Coffman, who settled at Smithfield, Pa. He had four sons and four daughters. One son, Henry, who married Elizabeth Robinson, settled on Robinson's Run, and acquired several hundred acres of land, did extensive farming and had a cooper shop; made barrels for the market. He had a saw mill nearby, and sawed his own materials. His wife was the daughter of Major Benjamin Robinson.

Henry Coffman was born in 1785, died November 12, 1862.

His children: 1, Felix, who married Martha Polly Stark. 2, Augustus W. 3, Jesse. 4, John G. 5, Benjamin R. 6, David. 7, Henry II. 8, George W. 9, Margaret. 10, Elizabeth.

We shall only make a record here of those who remained in this vicinity. John G. Coffman married February 15, 1838, Achsah Boggess, daughter of Alonzo Boggess.

Children of John and Achsah (Boggess) Coffman

1. Alonzo B., born, December 29, 1838, married, December 10, 1863, Emily Jane Harbert, daughter of Absalom Harbert.

2. Benjamin, born March 11, 1841, married Harriet Harbert, daughter of Absalom Harbert.

3. John Marshall, born May 15, 1843, married November 16, 1865, Clarissa Swiger.

4. Theophious, born May 27, 1845, killed in Jones' raid, Civil War, Fairmont, 1863.

5. Frederick, born June 21, 1847   6. Francis M., born June 26, 1849, both died young.

7. Jesse F., born, August 7, 1851, married November 2, 1872, Virginia Harbert, daughter of Seth Harbert.

8. Elizabeth, born August 16, 1853, married, October 11, 1877, Ferd Rogers, son of Lud Rogers.

9. Jasper, born, May 21, 1855.   10. Amenda, born, 1856, both died young.

11. Elmore Lee, born, July 13, 1857, married Francis Harbert.

12. Luther, born April 29, 1859, married November 6, 1884, Ida Cunningham. (See Mason genealogy.)

13. James T., born, May 27, 1861, married, Anne Shaw.

14. George, born, February 17, 1863, married Rosalie Weekly, daughter of Wm. Weekly.

15. Charles T., born, November 1, 1865, killed 1883 by a rolling log.

Children of John Marshall and Clarissa (Swiger) Coffman

1. Allison. 2, Seldon. 3, Charles G., married October 1909, Alma Haymaker.

He was an attorney, served as State Senator in 1909-1929. He was president of the Senate a part of this term.

4. Cora, married first October 9, 1901, to Leslie Hawker. (See Mason genealogy.)

Cora's children, Wayne and Marlin. She married second, Plummer Hill.

Children of Alonzo and Emily (Harbert) Coffman

1. Frederick. 2, W. Scott, married October 29, 1888, Mary V. Robey.
3. Sheridan. 4, Fillmore. 5, John.

J. H. Coffman, son of Scott and Mary V. Coffman married Bessie Smith.

Children of James and Anne (Shaw) Coffman.

1. Aubrey. 2, Stella. 3, Bertha. 4, Hugh, died aged 23, and Beryl. Aubrey married Florence Graham; his children, Lois and Charles. Beryl married April 15, 1917, Clyde Harbert, son of Charles and May (Griffin) Harbert.

Children of George and Rosalie (Weekly) Coffman.

1. Jessie, married June 2, 1917, Seward Hardesty, son of James Hardesty.

2. Aura, married June 1, 1913, John Earl Martin, son of Charles W. and Hattie Martin.

Jessie's children, Eleanor, Genevieve, Doris and James.

Aura's children, 1, Ruth, married Edward Nay. 2, Margaret. 3, George Lee.

Genevieve Hardesty married March 24, 1940, Russell

Curry, of Shinnston, W. Va., an electrician with the McAlpin Coal Co., Beckley, W. Va.

DENHAM GENEALOGY

David Denham married in 1805, Elizabeth Robinson, dauhter of McKinney and Elizabeth (Wamsley) Robinson. Monongalia county record show that one James Hall married in July 7, 1799, Hannah Denham, daughter of John Denham; surety, David Denham.

McKinney Robinson was a Revolutionary soldier.

Elizabeth Wamsley was a sister to David Wamsley, of the Big Elm farm, and to Dorcas Wamsley, wife of Solomon Shinn.

Claiborne Denham, son of David and Elizabeth (Robinson) Denham, married Mary Mason.. See Mason and Chalfant, March 26, 1840.

Dr. James Denham, son of David, married Rachel Flowers, daughter of Dr. Jesse and Mary (Lucas) Flowers.

Dr. James Denham's children: Syena, Miriam, Gwendolyn, Vesta, Sallie, James, Jr., and Dr. Cecil Denham, Effie. *and Columbia*

One John Denham was a Baptist minister in 1795. See Monongalia county marriage records.

DRUMMOND GENEALOGY. (SEE MARTIN)

Children of Clay and Carrie (Drummond) Davis

Raymond, married Elizabeth Shingleton.
Ralph, married Virginia Parsons.
Helen, married Glen Fortney, son of Lloyd Fortney.
Harold (Buck) married Ethel Lanham, daughter of John Lanham.
Roy, married Ardath Robinson, daughter of Carl Robinson (see Robinson genealogy).
Clay, Junior.

The Wilford Drummond family lived just over the hill from the Bartlett home toward Lumberport, on a part of the original Basil Lucas farm.

Mr. Drummond was a veteran of the Civil War, and lived to be quite old. He was an expert maker of hand wrought axe handles. We children used to love to watch him make those long, white shavings, then he would scrape with a piece of glass till the handle was smooth as polished marble. He used hickory wood.

Children of Clifton and Belle (Drummond) Lucas

Cordie, died in infancy. Flota, married, April 12, 1913, David Bice.
Fonda, married, November 27, 1920, Frank Phillips.
Jane, married, June 6, 1921, David Harris.
Franklin Niles, married, April 26, 1930, Wilma Hayes.
Gerald, married May 22, 1920, Catharine Heldreth, daughter of John Heldreth, of Shinnston.

Children of Arthur F. and Margaret (Sprout) Drummond.
Married April 1, 1900.

1. Ruby, born June 12, 1902. 2, Estelle, born September 21, 1911, married July 9, 1934 to Walter Glenn, Jr., born Januery 30, 1912. One son Walter Justus III, born January 29, 1940. The youngest person in this book.

Wilford and Jane Martin Drummond married November 26, 1868. Jane was the daughter of John and Elizabeth (Betsy) (Crim) Martin, married August 12, 1847, Harrison county.

The name Wilford Drummond appears as one of the earliest settlers around what is now Salem, W. Va., as early as 1793.

DUNCAN GENEALOGY

The family of John W. Duncan owned several acres just back of the church extending to the top of the hills on each side of the highway. His children were George, David, Asbury and others. Some of the Duncans married into the Ogden family but lived in another community. (See Ogden.)

Asbury remained here all his life and is buried in the family plot on the farm. He married Mary Ann Talkington, sister to Mrs. Van B. Ogden.

Children of Asbury and Mary (Talkington) Duncan

1. Abraham, born 1851, died 1856. 2. Malinda born 1852, died 1856.

3. Albert, born 1856, killed by auto 1937; married December 28, 1885 Jennie Wolford, daughter of Adam and Martha (Conaway) Wolford.

4. John, born 1857; married July 20, 1881, Susan Michael, sister to Mrs. D. Albert Hardesty.

5. Joseph Ezra, born 1865, married Mamie Barnes on March 26, 1893. Lives in Missouri and has one daughter who is a trained nurse.

Children of Albert and Jennie (Wolford) Duncan

1. Clarence, born 1886. 2. Ray, born 1887. 3. Ira, born 1889. 4. Bertice, born 1893. 5. Leo, born 1903. All live in Marshalltown, Iowa.

Children of John and Susan (Michael) Duncan

1. Forest, born 1882. He has one son, Harold and one grandson.
2. Charles, born 1884, died 1895. 3. Dallas, born 1892.

Asbury Duncan was a faithful attendant of the church and was class leader as long as he was physically able to go.

John Duncan's family went to Missouri about 1886. Ezra went in 1888. He married there, taught two years then went into the mercantile business.

Albert sold his farm to Solomon Chalfant and went west in 1890. Chalfant later sold it to Luther Piggott.

FLOWERS GENEALOGY

Members of the Flowers family came to America in the early 1700's and settled in Virginia. John Flowers came to Harrison county and married Sarah Barkley in 1800. He served in the war of 1812. He taught the "Loud School" mentioned on another page. His son, Dr. (Redhead) Jesse Flowers married Mary Lucas (born December 23, 1801). (See Lucas genealogy.)

Children of Dr. Jesse and Mary (Lucas) Flowers

1. Dr. Caleb married Naomi Fortney. 2. Rachel married Dr. James Denham.

2. Basil west to the middle west. Had a daughter Frances.

Children of Dr. Caleb and Naomi (Fortney) Flowers

1. John, married Ida McIntire.
2. Dr. Arthur O. married May Piggott, daughter of Elam Piggott. (See Piggott genealogy.) On daughter, Jane Flowers married ——— Stamm.
3. Dr. Newton E. One son Dr. Newton Earl, Jr., Clarksburg.
4. Viola, married Taylor Hess. Daughters, Laura and Pearl.
5. Elizabeth, married first, McIntire, daughter, Stella. Second, married Joshua Hess. Daughter, Bessie married Edgar Harmer. Jessie and others.
6. Belle married ——— Hustead, Sardis, W. Va.
7. Jennie married Grover Meeks
8. Kate married ——— Green.
9. Naomi married Sartoris Long, of Clarksburg. Went to Denver, Colorado.

Children of John and Ida (McIntire) Flowers

1. Ada, married James Green.
2. Bessie Jane, died in infancy.
3. Wiliam, married —— —Sturm, daughter of Frank and Allie Cunningham Sturm.
4. Charles, married ——— Sturm, sister to the above.
5. Ida, married ——— Riley.
6. Howard, Pittsburgh, Pa.

Lambert Flowers came from Maryland and bought 308 acres of land in 1798 from Wm. Robinson. It reached from Prospect Valley to the mouth of Piggott's Run. He was the great grandfather of Dr. Caleb Flowers.

HARBERT GENEALOGY

Three Harbert brothers came from Scotland and Ireland to Fort Pitt in 1745, namely, Jonathan, John, and Samuel. Jonathan started to return to Scotland, but was never heard of again.

John and Samuel settled in Washington county, Ohio. John was the father of Absalom who married an Allen. His children were Ai, Columbus, Luther, Mrs. Ben Coffman.

Samuel married Abigail Lusbury (Loughborough?)

Children of Samuel and Abigail Harbert

1. Thomas. 2. Edward or Ned, buried near Odell's Knob. (Monongalia county records in Morgantown, show one Edward Harbert married April 12, 1804, Elizabeth White.) 3. Samuel II, married Mary Thompson.

Children of Samuel II and Mary (Thompson) Harbert

1. Isaiah, married Orpha Shinn. 2. Jacky. 3. Nathan. 4. Samuel III.

5. Benjamin I, grandfather of Neaf, grandfather of Wid Harbert.

6. Sarah, married John Lewis Harvey.

7. Becky, married Bazil Harvey.

8. Betty, never married.

9. Ruhama, married first, a Corothers; second, a Starks on Tenmile Creek.

Children of Isaiah and Orpha (Shinn) Harbert)

1. Robert. 2, Seth, father of Rosetta, wife of Lemar Robinson. (See Robinson genealogy.)

2. Benjamin II, married Margaret Moore, daughter of Wm. Moore and Elizabeth (Hess) Moore, daughter of Jeremiah Hess I.

4. Lucinda, married Granville Boggess.

5. Rhoda, married Capt. James Moffatt.

6. Abigail, married Jeff Smith of Simpson's Creek.

Children of Benjamin II and Margaret (Moore) Harbert

1. Betty, married Gustavus Robey.
2. Sampson, married Rebecca Parsons; one daughter, Margaret.
3. Benjamin III, married Jane Moore.
4. Dora, married George Thompson.
5. Jim, married Grace Weese.
6. Frank, married Alice Virgis.
7. Jeremiah, married Elizabeth Monroe, daughter of J. Walker Monroe.
8. Ella, married first, Lawson Maulsby; second, Bud Ogden. One daughter, Lorna Maulsby, married Remmie Shreve, son of Adolphus Shreve. Remmie's one daughter, Alma.
9. Jacob, married Claudia Harbert, daughter of John Harbert.
10. Mary, married Isaac Ice.
11. Nathan, married Daisy Shreve, daughter of Adolphus Shreve. (See Shreve.)

Children of Benjamin III and Jane (Moore) Harbert

1. May, married Fletcher Piggott, son of Milton Piggott.
2. Benjamin IV, died young.
3. Leota, married Dorsey Robinson, son of Fletcher Robinson.
4. Agnes, married Benjamin Riley. 5. Gustavus, died young.
6. Wesley, married —— Goff.

Capt. James and Rhoda Harbert Moffatt had a son, George Moffatt, who married Mary Frances Keyser.

Children of George and M. Frances Moffatt

Peyton William, married Essie Martin. Florida, married John Stern. Martha, married Fred Meek, their son, George Meek, married Thelma Bostrom of Los Angeles,

Calif., chief wireless officer on the SS. President Cleveland of the Dollar line, now the American President line.

Dr. Benjamin Moffatt married Nell Hinebaugh, a nurse.

George Meek and Thelma Bostrom married April 7, 1935.

HARDESTY FAMILY GENEALOGY

James Hardesty lived on the north side of the river just west of Chiefton. His son John, was the father of John Hardesty, of Enterprise, Joseph, of Wyatt, and Mary Anne who married Asbury P. Sturm.

James Hardesty's son, Frank Hardesty, lived on what is known as Harbert's Run, on the land later owned by Benjamin Harbert, who sold it to A. W. Martin (see Piggott).

Children of Frank Hardesty

1. Mary Anne, married Lewis McIntire, of Worthington. (There were two Mary Annes.)

2. Rachel, married first, John Robinson; second, Asa Martin.

3. Rebecca, married Benjamin Coon. 4, James. 5, Thomas. 6, Charles Thornton who traveled all over the world, and was once a member of the State Legislature of Colorado.

7. Washington was drowned in the West Fork River when he fell out of a boat. He no doubt was injured in the fall, for he had always been a good swimmer. You will find the names of these children on the early Sunday school rolls.

Children of Lewis and Mary Anne (Hardesty) McIntire

1. Thornton Fleming (Stone), married first, Lucy McDannold; second, wife Rosalie (Tattie) Martin. 3, Belle Shaw.

2. Everal McIntire, married May Nixon. (See Lucas.)

3. Isaac, married Hattie Tetrick, daughter of Barney Tetrick. 4, Luella, married Dr. Howell.

Frank Hardesty with all his family, except Mary Anne and Rachel, later moved to Ritchie county, where he lived to a ripe old age. He was murdered by an insane stepdaughter.

Seward Hardesty, who lives at the present time on the original John Chalfant farm, is a grandson of Joseph Hardesty, of Wyatt. (See Coffman genealogy.)

The David Albert Hardesty family who were so closely associated with the life of the author of this chronicle, lived on the high hill between the upper valley and Lumberport. You will find them twining as a binding cord throughout this narrative. We were playmates.

Children of David Albert and Mary (Michael) Hardesty

Emma Delilah, married Edward Rowan, of Roquefort, Colo., one daughter, Marguerite

Erlen B. (He is to be credited for getting us enthused to begin collecting data for this book.)

Edgar, married Mattie Davidson. He is a member of the Rhinehart and Dennis Construction Co., of Charlottesville, Va. Has one daughter, Edith.

Florence died rather young.

Elsie, married December 24, 1912, Rev. Harry W. Flanagan.

Anna, married Chester Martin, principal of Wyatt, W. Va. high school. One son Philip.

Children of Rev. Harry W. and Elsie (Hardesty) Flanagan

1. Mary Virginia, born July 10, 1915.
2. James Erlen, born January 23, 1921.

3. Miriam Alice, born December 9, 1923.

Mary Hardesty Michael was the daughter of Henry and Rose Anne Michael who lived at Ida May. His parents were Irish, and originally spelled their name McMichael. They lived at Barracksville and were the founders of the Baptist church of that place.

Anna Hardesty was born September 12, 1888; married August 7, 1919.

David Albert and Mary Michael Hardesty, married November 13, 1873. (See Michael-Hawker.)

HAWKER GENEALOGY

One William Hawker and his wife, Margaret, came from Ireland shortly previous to the Revolutionary War and settled at or near Baltimore for a short time, and later went to Kentucky. They both died there sometime in the 1780's, leaving three children, Margaret, Amos, and Owen who was born March 15, 1775.

Not long after the death of their parents, the children found their way back to their relatives at Baltimore. There the boys were apprenticed to planters. Owen was at that time about 17 years of age, soon became dissatisfied, and joined an emigrant train to Winchester, Va., settled permanently there. He followed the profession of teaming, hauling goods to points farther west, sometimes as far as Kentucky and Tennessee. About 1800 he married at Bunker Hill, Berkeley county, Va., Mary Dunn, a daughter of James and Sarah (Reed) Dunn. This couple, with her parents, were included in a caravan that left that section in 1805 bound for Monongalia county; they made their settlement on West Run, about one mile above where Easton now stands. In 1807 he purchased 79 acres of land, built himself a two-room cabin and later as the family increased, added two more to it, remained there until 1845 when he sold his farm and bought 100 acres on Dent's Run, four miles west of Morgantown, where he and his wife made their home with their son, Owen, Jr., until their deaths. He died September 22, 1853, the wife died February 27, 1871.

James, fifth child of Owen and Mary (Dunn) Hawker are the ancestors of the Hawkers in this vicinity. James Hawker, born February 11, 1811, died November 8, 1894; married September 8, 1842, Elizabeth Michael Fletcher, widow of Amon Fletcher. She was born June 5, 1815, died September 21, 1892, daughter of John and Selah (Wade) Michael. See Franklin Brand's history of the Wade family.

Thomas Hawker, fifth child of James and Elizabeth (Michael) Hawker, born June 1, 1846, died October 10, 1921, married September 27, 1874, Amanda Mason, born December 15, 1849. (See Mason genealogy.) Died March 31, 1940.

Jane, seventh child of James and Elizabeth, born May 1, 1851, died January 8, 1886, married November 26, 1868, James A. Robinson, he died December 17, 1926. (See Robinson genealogy.)

LUCAS FAMILY GENEALOGY

Part of this is copied from "Clarksburg Exponent-Telegram" dated Sunday, March 25, 1934, however I have made some verified corrections.

Pension records of Virginia, published in 1835 show that one Basil Lucas, of Frederick county, Virginia, was listed as a Revolutionary pensioner, having been a sergeant in the Virginia militia, and having enlisted for four years in the Maryland Continental line. His war record says he was born in 1757, and died in 1841. My correction is—This could not be the same Basil.

Comparing dates, we find that our ancestor Basil was born February, 1738 and died March 25, 1820.

His first wife, the mother of Basil's only child, John Deakins Lucas, may have been a Deakins, John D. Lucas was born July 3, 1769,, died December 30, 1847. The above dates are in the Lucas family Bible.

Monongalia county records show that Basil did not marry Joanna Chipps till December 17, 1805. John D. was then 36 years old, and only 12 years younger than the Revolutionary soldier.

Harrison county records show that Basil bought some land about that time from a William Chipps.

The soldier Basil left a widow, Elizabeth, and a daughter, Tabitha, who married William Cosley in 1801.

John Deakins Lucas married on June 6, 1796, Jane Renicks; she was born September 22, 1775, died between 1806 and 1813. His second wife was Mary Nixon, no children. John D. and Jane Renicks Lucas had six children (1) Amelia, (2) Basil, who never married, (3) William (ancestor of Melville Bartlett's family and of Luther and Jane (Lucas) Harbert's family), (4) Mary Poppy, married Dr. Jesse Flowers, (5) John Hooker, went west (6) George R., father of Rawley, Edward and William Lucas. The 600 acres he bought from William Robinson on June 18, 1798, reached from Piggott's Run to the West Fork River. The house was torn down about 1935.

John Deakins Lucas' son, William, married, first, Unity Shinn, April 15, 1822, daughter of Solomon and Dorcas (Wamsley) Shinn.

William's children by first marriage (1) Elizabeth, married Absalom Bartlett, (2) Thomas, married Amelia Metz, (3) George, went to Kansas, (4) Saul, married Polly Coon, (5), Basil, died young.

William Lucas' second wife was Minerva Shinn, married February 16, 1847, daughter of Benjamin and Mary (Shinn) Shinn. She was a niece of Unity.

His only child by the second marriage was Jane Lucas, who married Luther Harbert. (See family elsewhere).

Children of Elizabeth and Absalom Bartlett (1) Melville B., married Christena Chalfant, (2) Sarah Jane, married Jesse Martin, (3) Hannah Unity (Hattie), died young. See elsewhere for Melville B.'s family.

Only child of Saul Lucas, Angeline, married Bud Ogden.

Children of Thomas and Amelia Metz Lucas (1) Louisa Ann, married William Harrison. Louisa's children: Hattie, married Fred Martin, Charles, Archie, and Jesse. (2) B. Frank Lucas, son of Thomas Lucas, married Jane Bock. Their children (1) Clifton Basil, married Belle Drummond, (2) Thomas E., married Ella Ashcraft, (3) Blanche, married James Heldreth, (4) Daisy, married a Matheney.

Mary (Poppy), daughter of John D. Lucas, married Dr. Jesse Flowers. Their children (1) Basil, married Mary Ann Baker, daughter of Joe Baker. They had one daughter, Frances, and later went to Holden, Missouri, (2) Caleb (Doctor), married on August 12, 1851, Naomi Fortney, daughter of Jacob Fortney of Lumberport. Dr. Jesse Flowers' daughter, Rachel, married Dr. James Denham. Dr. Jesse Flowers' second wife was Roanna Cunningham.

George Renicks Lucas, youngest son of J. Deakins Lucas, married, in 1830, Amelia Sibba Rogers, daughter of Edward and Elizabeth Wood Rogers, who were also pioneers, the former born July 22, 1785, and the latter June 27, 1782, and married February 5, 1805, at Clarksburg by Rev. George Towers.

Brothers and sisters of Sibba Rogers Lucas are as follows: William Harrison Rogers, John Wood Rogers, Dudley E. Rogers, Rawley George Rogers, Lucien Payne Rogers, Solomon Wood Rogers, Julia Helen Rogers, Frances Margaret and Elizabeth Marian Rogers.

Children of George R. and Amelia Rogers Lucas (1) William, married Mrs. Mary Lowe, (2) Amanda, married John Marshall Boggess, (3) Mary, married Elkanah Davis, (4) Edward, married Minerva Chalfant, (5) (5) Amelia (Daught), married William Nixon, (6) Rawley George, married Mary Chalfant, (7) Martha, married Marion Vincent.

Rawley's children, John R., Joseph, and Basil H.

Amanda Lucas Boggess children, Charles, Basil, "Sis," George and Lee Boggess.

Lee Boggess married Grace Barnes, their children, Carney Boggess, Sydney Boggess, Beulah Boggess, who married Dr. Coffindaffer.

John Marshall Boggess was a son of George Washington Boggess and Malinda Robinson Boggess, who was a daughter of Major Benjamin Robinson and Mary Margaret Asson Boggess.

Children of William and Amelia Lucas Nixon: George Nixon, married Pearl Bartlett, daughter of Cree Bartlett.

George's children, Ruth, Roy, Beatrice, Harry, Lee, William, Robert.

These Nixon children are becoming scientific farmers and at an early age have won many prizes and scholarships for their splendid work and fine live stock.

May Nixon married Everal McIntire, son of Louis and Mary Ann (Hardesty) McIntire.

John R. Lucas (son of Rawley), for a number of years has conducted a riding school of state-wide renown, on the site of the Flowers farm near the reservoir dam.

He also owned a fine race horse stallion "Directum I." This horse held eight world records for speed; and was a thoroughbred of most royal ancestry. A descendant of (1) "Director," winner of the Charter Oak $10,000 purse, (2) "Dictator," (3) "Pactolus," (4) "Patronage," and (5) the $28,000 "Pancoast."

(See Chalfant genealogy for the Rawley Lucas family.)

Major Benjamin Robinson was married at least three times.

1. Mary Wilkinson May 19, 1785.

2. Nancy Webb, in 1816, mother of Mrs. Henry Coffman.

3. Mary Asson Boggess, mother of Malinda Robinson Boggess, who was the mother of John Marshall Boggess.

MARTIN GENEALOGY

John F. Martin, married Elizabeth (Betsy) Crim, daughter of Peter Crim.

Children of John F. and Betsy (Crim) Martin

1. Richard Owen, married Jane Ashcraft, daughter of "Little Zeke" Ashcraft.

2. Rutha Jane, born 1852, married 1868, Wilford Drummond, born 1830 on Lambert's Run, son of Pendleton and Naomi Hutson Drummond, married September 4, 1819.

Children of Wilford and Rutha Jane (Martin) Drummond

1. Francis, killed by a train near Clarksburg.

2. Arthur F., married Margaret Jane Sprout, daughter of Isaac and Louisa Sprout. Arthur's children: 1, Ruby 2, Estelle, married Walter Glenn.

3. Cora Belle, married Clifton B. Lucas, son of Frank Lucas. (See Drummond.)
4. Amanda, married Lloyd Fortney.
5. Carrie, married Clay Davis.

Children of Richard Owen and Jane (Ashcraft) Martin

1. Russell, married first, Bird Lindsey, daughter of Matt Lindsey; second, Caroline Lipscomb. 2, Charles, never married.
3. Wilmer, married Mary Cunningham. (See Burns.)
4. John, married Amanda Odell; children, Nile and Arnold.
Cecil, Della, Albert, Mamie, Nellie, Carl married Kate Starkey, Christena Jane married Clint Dawson.

Children of Russell and Bird (Lindsey) Martin, first wife

Jennie May, Ailsa Jane, Goldie, Richard, Clinton and Laura.

Dorothy Martin, daughter of Russell and Caroline (Lipscomb) Martin, married Glen Grose. Their children, Pauline, Mack, Jessie, Mary Ellen, William George, Glenn Wayne, Dorothy and Edward.

Carl Martin's children, Kelsie, Pauline, and Freeman. Freeman died aged 10.

Children of Russell and Maud (Odell) Martin, second wife

1. Alice, married Earl Wilson. One child, Donald Richard.
2. Loraine. 2, Thelma, married Ruben Varco.

MARTIN GENEALOGY

Children of Charles H. and Pidge (Martin) McNemar

1, James R. 2, Jeannette, married Wm. Shreve. 3, Linnie, married Edw. Carrico.

4. Andrew. 5, Geneva, married Alvis Kisner. One child, Delores Jean Kisner.

6. Rebecca. 7, Naomi. 8, Charles, Jr. 9. Willard. 10, Ruth. 11, Eleanora. 12, Iahmael, married Geneva Harrison. One child, Joyce Anne McNemar.

Children of Edward and Linnie (McNemar) Carrico

1. Charles Edward. 2, Richard. 3, Verna Jane.

Peter Crim, born 1797, died December 13, 1864, married Susan (Nay) Crim who was born 1797, died October 30, 1856. Their children: 1, Fielding, married first Mary Cunningham who died April 24, 1851. His second wife was Elizabeth Martin, born 1841, married October 8, 1858, daughter of Daniel and Nancy (Bland) Martin.

2. Elizabeth Crim, married first, John F. Martin; second, Bert Drummond.

MASON GENEALOGY

(Courtesy of F. W. Cunningham)

Somewhere east of the Allegheny mountains, one Robert Mason was born March 31, 1781, died January 25, 1871.

He married August 4, 1814, Rebecca Hall, daughter of Asa and Sophia (White) Hall.

Asa Hall was the son of Thomas and Rebecca (Storey) Hall. Thomas Hall was born in 1724, at Duck Creek, Delaware.

Children of Robert, Sr. and Rebecca (Hall) Mason

1. Daniel Mason, born October 29, 1815, married, first, Malinda Robinson, November 15, 1838; second Sarah Young, April 5, 1871.

2. Robert, Jr., born April 10, 1817, died March 10, 1877, married March 22, 1843, Rebecca Robinson, daughter of John and Rebecca Wamsley Robinson (Mason genealogy.)

3. Mary, born November 20, 1818, married March 26, 1840, to Clabe Denham.

4. Peter, born March 19, 1820, married Tobitha Shinn October 14, 1841.

5. John, born September 22, 1821, married October 13, 1842, Mary Jane Richardson.

Children of Daniel and Malinda (Robinson) Mason

1. Charles Wesley, died in infancy.

2. John R., born October 11, 1839, married December 9, 1850, Mary Ann Rusk.

3. Martha Ann Mason, born November 20, 1842, married February 1, 1866, John Hawker, son of James Hawker of Hessville.

4. George Mason, born July 24, 1845, married Annie Shears; went to Illinois.

5. Mary E. Mason, born October 9, 1847, married September 5, 1867, to Stephen Brown.

Children of Daniel and Sarah (Young) Mason, second wife

1. Ida Mason, born April 4, 1873, married Lyda Robinson, son of Dudley Robinson.

2. Daniel Ellis, born May 19, 1875, went to Sistersville.

Children of Robert Mason, Jr. and Rebecca (Robinson) Mason

1. Amanda, married September 27, 1874, Thomas Hawker, son of James Hawker, Sr.

2. Sarah Florence, married Mahlon Harbert.
3. Albert Mason, married Amenda Shreve.
4. Effie, married March 26, 1885, E. M. (Bel) Hess.

Children of Mary and Claiborne Denham

1. Martha, married Thornton Martin.
2. Mary Denham, married March 6. 1861, William Chalfant, son of John Chalfant.
3. Robert Denham, married 1872, Mary Armstrong. Robert's son, Charles, married Pearl Willis.

Children of John and Jane (Richardson) Mason

The only members of this family who were at any time connected with this community are the following:

Mary Mason, married Dudley Robinson.

Emily Mason, married Frederick Cunningham.

R. Ellis Mason, married Elfie Robinson, daughter of John R. and Caroline Boggess Robinson.

R. Ellis Mason was a singing master and conducted a singing school in Prospect Valley. He also brought the entire Sunday school of Indian Run to Chalfant's Grove once back in the 1880's, and gave one of the finest Children's Day programs ever heard.

Children of Ellis and Elfie R. Mason

1. Arnold.
2. Emsie, married Last Post (Raymond and Sylvia). Lives in Detroit, Mich.
3. Launa married Ed Deveny, son of Michael Deveny.
4. Wilbur married Willa Bowman, twins, Robert Lewis and Maralyn, born March 8, 1939, at Charleston, W. Va.

Children of Frederick and Emily (Mason) Cunningham

1. Ida Cunningham, married November 6, 1884, Luther Coffman. Has one daughter, Desie Coffman, married Ed. V. Richardson. Their daughter, Jean.
2. Allie Cunningham, married November 16, 1886,

Frank Sturm. Had three children, Ernie, married William Flowers, Arlie married Charles Flowers. Glen Sturm married Grace Jones. William and Charles were sons of John F. and grandsons of Dr. Caleb Flowers.

3. Chester C., married March 12, 1896, Alvena Robinson, daughter of Thaddeus Robinson. Two children, Castle and Ruth. Chester's second wife, Linnie Brake, one daughter.

4. Howard C., married November 23, 1896, Mabel Boggess, daughter of Bruce Boggess.

5. Willard C., married October 24, 1897, Rosetta Robinson, daughter of Thaddeus Robinson.

6. Gilmer C., married September 27, 1905, Alma Hardesty, daughter of James Hardesty.

7. Byron C. married Willa Riggs September 24, 1908, has one daughter, Mary.

Children of Mahlon and Florence (Mason) Harbert

1. Guy Harbert. 2, Lorna, married J. Amos Robinson, son of James Robinson. (See Robinson genealogy).

Children of Albert and Amanda (Shreve) Mason

1. Carma, married Essel M. Robinson. 2, Ocie, married Carl Robinson.

3. Virgil, married Eva Robinson, (See Robinson genealogy.)

4. Guy, married Lulu Martin.

Children of Thomas and Amanda (Mason) Hawker

1. Leslie, married Cora Coffman, daughter of John Marshall Coffman. Leslie's children, Wayne and Marlen. Leslie was killed in an automobile acident September 15, 1912.

2. Lelia Hawker, married Marshall W. Ogden. (See Ogden genealogy.)

3. Stella, married Clarence W. Nutter. Stella's children, Julia, Margaret, Ardis and Avis. The latter are twins.

4. Dallas Hawker, married, first, Blanche Berry, died without children; second Icie Kinkead, November 27, 1909. Dallas' children, Max Mason, Virginia, Juanita, and Thomas.

5. Homer Hawker, married Linda Rohrbough. One daughter, Josephine.

Leslie Hawker founded the Hawker Hardware company in Shinnston, it is still owned and operated by the Hawker heirs.

Children of E. M. and Effie (Mason) Hess

1. Bessie, married Fred Reger.
2. Argyl, married Lacie Robinson. (See Robinson genealogy.)

MICHAEL GENEALOGY

For a more extensive research on the Michaels, see Franklin Brand's History of the Wade Family. Harrison county's records show that Paul Michael bought 321 acres on Mill Fall Run in 1807. His wife was named Sarah ———. Their sons: 1, John. 2, Henry. 3, David. Henry is also listed as "Mike," married Hannah Cambpell, February 18, 1806. He was a Revolutionary soldier on Capt. Nathaniel Cochran's muster roll.

John, son of Paul and Sarah Michael, died August 23, 1870, married January 12, 1812; Selah Wade, born November 1, 1791, died July 3, 1835 in Harrison county.

OGDEN GRIST MILL

Children of John and Selah (Wade) Michael

1. Elizabeth, (see Hawker genealogy).
2. Henry born November 20, 1820, died May 16, 1863, married in Marion county, Anna Clelland, she died December 3, 1862, daughter of Patrick Clelland.

Children of Henry and Anna C. Michael

1. Alexander, (see Brand's History of Wade family).
2. Mary Michael, born June 25, 1855, married November 13, 1873, D. Albert Hardesty. (See Hardesty genealogy.)
3. Susan, (see Duncan genealogy).

THE OGDEN GRIST MILL

Mr. Harvey W. Harmer in his "History of Harrison County Mills," has ably told the origin and various owners, so I shall only tell of its location; with the help of Marshall Ogden's sketch from memory I have made a pencil drawing which he says is a fair representation of how it looked. It was located a short distance below the present reservoir. Those are two of the Ogden boys playing in the tree, but each of you readers may name for yourself which of your ancestors is on his way to the mill. He is wearing his newest linsey-woolsey "wampus" that his wife spun and made for him.

OGDEN GENEALOGY

Jonathan Ogden, the first ancestor of record, resided near Port Tobacco, Md., and is believed to be a lineal descendant, in the fifth generation, of the Pilgrim, John Ogden, who was born in Bradley Plains, Hampshire, England, September 19, 1609; came to America in 1640 to the southern shore of Long Island.

Jonathan Ogden, married Anne Howell, of Howell's Delight; daughter of Paul and Mary Howell. They were the parents of the following children:

1. Tobitha, born September 17, 1767, married Uzza Barnes.

2. William Rhodey I, born October 16, 1769, married 1806, April 5, Phoebe Hall.

3. Mary, born January 15, 1772, married Jeremiah Robey in Maryland.

4. Thomas, born September 20, 1775, died April 12, 1830, married 1793, Elizabeth Moore, born August 5, 1775.

5. Sarah, born May 5, 1778, married Michael Martin in Maryland. 6, Samuel, born February, 1781, died in Maryland. 7, Nathan, born April 15, 1783, married Eleanor Kidwell in Maryland.

8. Susannah, born October 11, 1785, married Mark Bigler.

9. Nancy Ann, born April 25, 1788, married John Richardson in Maryland.

10. Elizabeth, born November 22, 1790, no record.

Thomas, son of Jonathan and Ann (Howell) Ogden, was born September 30, 1775, came to Enterprise with his parents and lived on the eastern bank of the West Fork River below Enterprise. Was a successful trader and accumulated considerable real and personal property. He married Elizabeth Moore in Maryland.

Children of Thomas and Elizabeth (Moore) Ogden

1. Mary, died in infancy. 2. Anne, married Nathaniel Barnes.

3. William mentioned below; born September 24, 1802, married Sally McIntire.

4. Samuel, born August 4, 1809, married April 17, 1831, Julia Duncan.

5. Nathan, mentioned below, born June 14, 1811, married April 17, 1831, Jane Duncan.

6. Jonathan, born October 10, 1814, married Emily Duncan. 7. Benjamin, born November 3, 1806, died in infancy.

These Duncan girls were all sisters to Asbury Duncan.

Thomas Ogden's will dated April 7, 1830, is recorded in Harrison county, as is also the will of his father, Jonathan Ogden, made August 13, 1807. Nathan, son of Thomas and Elizabeth (Moore) Ogden, was a lumber and grain merchant, shipping down the river from the old boat yard at the mouth of Robinson's Run, about which more is told on another page of this book. He was a Whig and a Methodist.

Children of Nathan and Jane (Duncan) Ogden

1. Thomas Alfred, died in infancy. 2. Van Buren, mentioned below.

3. Thomas Jefferson, married Ella Varner. Parents of Wayman and Rosa Ogden.

Wayman Ogden married Rachel Cousins, of Hadley, Pa., while she was teaching Spanish in South American schools. Rosa married Rev. John Haines, of Colorado Springs, Colorado.

4. Serena married Charles Daugherty. They were the parents of Charles, Jr., Icie, and Ina Daugherty. Ina married Samuel Weekly.

Van B. Ogden, second son of Nathan and Jane Duncan Ogden, was born November 27, 1837, died January 28,

1911. He followed the trade of blacksmith till 1873, later he made boots and shoes, and was a merchant in Prospect Valley with Benjamin Harbert. Their store burned; then they built a brick one. It is still being used for a dwelling.

He was made postmaster by President U. S. Grant, and served till 1904 when R. F. D. was established. He married September 29, 1864, Marcy Ellen Talkington, born February 27, 1835, in Marion county, W. Va., daughter of Abraham and Elizabeth (Hartley) Talkington.

Children of Van B. Ogden

1. Sarah Janie, born January 28, 1866, married Derry Shreve, died June 4, 1889.

2. William Burtice, born April 13, 1867, a prominent educator, died unmarried April 7, 1893.

3. Ellsworth E., born October 19, 1869, married May 16, 1893, Lillie Weekly, daughter of Wm. Weekly.

4. Emma Z., born August 21, 1874, married December 21, 1893, J. David Robinson. (See Robinson.)

5. Marshall W. born January 26, 1875, married Lelia Hawker June 16, 1901.

(See Mason and Hawker genealogy for Marshall Ogden's family.)

Children of Ellsworth and Lillie (Weekly) Ogden

1. Paul, born December 15, 1895. 2, Ira, born July 25, 1897. 3, William, born October 12, 1899.

4. Zabel Flora, born March 5, 1905. 5, Maxon, married Ruby Sandy.

(For children of David and Emma (Ogden) Robinson, (see Robinson genealogy).

Son of Marshall and Lelia Hawker Ogden. (See Mason)

Leland, married Kathryn Breneman.

Twin daughters of Leland and Kathryn Ogden, Sherry Leonard and Sandra Lee.

VAN B. OGDEN FAMILY

Son of Maxon and Ruby (Sandy) Ogden, Howard Ellery Ogden.

Family of Presley B. Ogden

Dr. Presley B. Ogden, fifth son of William and Sallie (McIntire) Ogden, grandson of Thomas and Elizabeth Moore Ogden and great grandson of Jonathan and Ann Howell Ogden, was born April 29, 1837, married first, August 26, 1863, in Monongalia county, Mary Coombs, born December 4, 1837, daughter of Phillip and Elizabeth (Pindall) Coombs; second wife, Alice M. Sapp. Phillip Coombs born January 22, 1785. Elizabeth Pindall, born February 17, 1798.

Dr. P. B. Ogden was a physician in Fairmont, W. Va. Was assistant surgeon under Colonel D. D. Johnson in the Civil War.

Children

1. Howard, married Olive Mayers June 2, 1889.
    Children:
    1. Marjorie, married Oscar L. Stanard.
       Children:
       1. Ella Jean, born July 18, 1914.
       2. Shirley, J., born June 17, 1917, married 1939, Daniel K. Swihart.
    2. Alma, born August 26, 1891, married Erwin F. Plumb, November, 1916.
       Children:
       1. Virginia F., born July 23, 1918, married September 1939, Philip White.
       2. Priscilla, born October 31, 1923.
       3. Ogden, T., born May, 1929.
    3. Dana Presley, married Vera Gasman, July, 1923.
       Children:
       1. Dana P., Jr.
       2. Mary Elizabeth.
    4. Josephine, born July 7, 1899, married James V. Forrestal.

Children:
1. Michael O., born 1928.
2. Peter Ogden, born 1930.
2. Dr. William C., married Emma Post, sister of Melville Davidson Post, a short-story writer.
No children.
3. Herschel, born Jan. 12, 1869, married Mary Moorhouse of Brownsville, Pa. Educated in public schools at Fairmont, graduated Fairmont State Normal and State University. Began newspaper work in Wheeling 1887. Publisher of Wheeling News-Register, Wheeling Intelligencer and a number of other newspapers in West Virginia.
Children:
1. Frances. Married D. W. Stubblefield.
Children:
1. Frances.
2. Anne.
3. Margaret. (Live in Charleston, W. Va.)
2. Margaret. Married George Nutting, of Hinton, W. Va. Doctor in Washington, D. C.
4. Cora. Married Winfield H. Spragg, 1905. Born 1870.
No children.

PIGGOTT GENALOGY

This first paragraph is from Hardesty's History of Harrison and Marion Counties.

"Dr. Edward Piggott came from England prior to the Revolutionary War, and settled in what is now New

HERSCHEL C. OGDEN, Publisher

Jersey. One of his brothers was in the battle of Bunker Hill. Edward's son, George settled at Cumberland, Md., and George's son, Jesse, came to Harrison county, Va., in 1808. Jesse Piggott married Anna Heldreth March 8, 1810. She was the daughter of Frazier Heldreth, whose ancestors came from New Castle, Pa., and were of English and French descent. Frazier Heldreth's wife was Rebecca Jacquet. Jesse died May 3, 1829, leaving four sons and four daughters. 1, Jesse II, 2, Milton, 3, George, 4, Seth."

Another record says Mary, daughter of George Piggott, married May 23, 1811, Aaron Shinn, son of Levi and Elizabeth (Smith) Shinn, who built the stone house in Shinnston. His daughter, Phoebe Piggott, married John W. Duncan.

Jesse II and Milton remained on Piggott's Run. George went to Dola, and Seth went to Sardis.

Jesse II married Emma Hall. Milton married Dorcas Jones.

Children of Jesse and Emma (Hall) Piggott.

1. Elam, born 1839, married Amanda Boggess, daughter of John W. Boggess.

2. Jane, married Lamar Cunningham. 3. Eliza, never married.

4. Golden Thomas, a doctor. 5. Luther, 6. Fidella.

Elam lived on Bingamon, near Wyatt. Their children, 1, Chester, married Carrie Randall; 2, May, married Dr. Arthur Flowers; 3, Effie, married Omar Swiger; 4, Ernest, married Bertha Hardesty, daughter of Joseph and Louisa Hardestey; 5, Wilbur, Clarksburg druggist; 6, Luther.

Milton Piggott, born October 23, 1828, married August 31, 1851 Dorcas Jones, born February, 1833.

Children of Milton and Dorcas (Jones) Piggott

1, William Elmer, born June 28, 1852; 2, E. Marshall; 3, Luther; 4, Lloyd; 5, John W.; 6, Jane; 7, Benjamin F.;

8, Charles; 9, Arthur; 10, Fletcher; 11, Ellis; 12, Clara; 13, Floe E.; 14, Herbert.

Elmer married Almeda Martin, daughter of Dorsey Martin. Marshall married a Shreves. Jane married Adolphus Shreve. Fletcher married May Harbert, daughter of Benjamin Harbert. Clara married Homer Michael, lives in Urbana, Ohio, has one son, Brooks. He married Louise ———, has one child, Rebecca Jane.

Floe married Otto Martin, son of William Martin of Pine Bluff.

Herbert married a Matheny.

Children of Otto and Floe (Piggott) Martin

1, Neil, married Emzie Robinson, daughter of Essel Robinson; 2, Blair, married Georgie Blocher; 3, Nellie, married ——— Merrifield; 4, Pauline, married Bernard Odell; 5, Wayne, married Delano Carrico; 6, June; 7, Dorcas.

The Piggott's have all made their homes elsewhere except Mr. and Mrs. Otto Martin. They own and occupy the Harbert farm.

The original Piggott home is now the home of Mr. and Mrs. Thos Carrico whose children are: 1, Irene, married Wayne Ashcraft; 2, Delano, married Wayne Martin; 3, Estes.

Luther Piggott married Mary Wolford. Their children Howard, Homer, and Garrett. Howard married Hattie Nutter. Homer married Mary Minnich, daughter of Andrew Minnich, and had one daughter, Lucy Piggott. Piggott's bought the Duncan fram.

ROBINSON GENEALOGY

See the first pages of this book for the earlier generations of Robinson. We give here only those whose descendants remained in this community, namely: David and George, who were sons of John and Rebecca (Wamsley) Robinson. David was sheriff of Harrison county during the Civil War.

David married Mary Cunningham, sister to Fred W. Cunningham.

Childrn of David and Mary (Cunningham) Robinson

1, Verna, married Edward Denham, her children, Sherman, Dora, and John Denhom.

2. James A., married Jane Hawker, sister to Thomas Hawker.

Children of James and Jane (Hawker) Robinson

1, David, married December 21, 1893, Emma Z. Ogden, daughter of V. B. Ogden.

2, Cecil, married Frances Griffin.   3, Betty, married Colfax McCarty.

4, Carrie, married Alden Sprout, son of Isaac and Louisa Sprout.

5, Amos, married Lorna Harbert, daughter of Mahlon and Florence (Mason) Harbert.

6, Henry, married Elsie Hardesty, daughter of James Hardesty.   7, Nellie.

Children of David and Emma Robinson.

1, Wayman, married Willa, daughter of Francis Robinson of Lumberport.

2, Vera, teacher in Lumberport schools.

Children of Wayman and Willa Robinson.   1, Virginia Lee; 2, Rhoda; 3, Marjorie Ann; 4, Ellen.

Children of Cecil and Frances (Griffin) Robinson

1, Edward, married Alma Fortney. Their children,

Marcella Jane and Darrell; 2, Kenneth, married Pauline Sturm; 3, Glen.

Children of Colfax and Betty (Robinson) McCarty.

1, Clyde, married Freda Nuzum.

2. Omar, married Elsie Fortney.

Children of Omar: Esther June, married Glen Watkins, Maxine, Betty Jane, Dorothea, Opal, J. Wayne, and Dolores.

Children of Lawrence: Kenneth, James, and Donald Lyle.

Children of Alden and Carrie (Robinson) Sprout.

1. Esrom, married Ruby Malone. 2, Herman, married Reva Cobb.

Son of Amos and Lorna (Harbert) Robinson.

Ray, married Ida Parkey; their children, Anna Lorna and Betty Ray.

Children of Henry and Elsie (Hardesty) Robinson

1. Dr. Dennis; 2, Margaret; 3, Ruth Eleanor.

Lamar, son of George and Amelia (Boggess) Robinson, married Rozetta Harbert, daughter of Seth Harbert.

Children of Lamar and Rozetta (Harbert) Robinson

1, Gracie, married Emory Cunningham, son of William Cunningham.

2, Essel, married March, 1901, Carma Mason (see Mason genealogy.)

3, Carl, married October 20, 1901, Ocie Mason (see Mason genealogy.)

4, Eva, married Virgil Mason (see Mason genealogy.)

5, Lacie, married Argyl Hess.

Children of Emory and Gracie (Robinson) Cunningham

1, Arlie; 2, Orsie; 3, Erma; 4, Clyde; 5, Garnet; 6, Dennis.

Children of Essel and Carma (Mason) Robinson

1, Beulah, married Vance Anderson; 2, Emsie, married Neil Martin, one daughter, Joan; 3, Bertha, married Andy Silisky; 4, Walter, married Virginia Thornberg.

Children of Virgil and Eva (Robinson) Mason

1, Jewel, married Charlie Hayhurst; 2, Dale, married Marie Nutter. Daughter, Shirley Ann; son, Ronald N.; 3, Vesta Lee.

Children or Argyl and Lacie (Robinson) Hess

1, Wilma, married Tommy Kesling; 2, Paul, married Carol Swiger; 3, Geo. Robert.

Children of Carl and Ocie (Mason) Robinson

1, Hudson, married Elizabeth Goodman; 3, Willis; 4, Edith, married Jay Westfall; 5, Ardath, married Ray Davis, son of Clay and Carrie (Drummond) Davis. Hudson's children, John and Waverly Hale.

ROGERS GENEALOGY

Children of Rhodam and Mildred (Nelson) Rogers

1, Rhodam E; 2, Peyton Taylor, married Ruth Corneilson; 3, Ludwell, father of Ferd and Marietta; 4, Elizabeth, married —— Cuningham; 5, Eunice; 6, Sarah, married —— Shrader; 7, Eva, married Benjamin Harvey.

Ferd Rogers married Elizabeth Coffman (see Coffman). Their children: 1, Bernard; 2, Ada; 3, Ray.

Marietta married Millard Gore. Their children: 1,

Dr. Truman Gore; 2, Ferd, a stockman and farmer; 3, Claude, attorney at law; 4, Howard M. Gore, Ex-Governor of West Virginia.

SHREVE FAMILY GENEALOGY

The first Shreve of which there is authenticated record was Sir William Shreve, from southeastern part of Europe, who married Elizabeth Farfax, Lady Elizabeth, tradition states. They had a son, William, who married a lady of Amsterdam by the singular name of Ora Ora, the daughter of a wealthy nobleman. After their marriage they came came to Portsmouth, R. I. They had two sons, Caleb and John.

Caleb Shreve received warrants for land in East New Jersey from proprietors as early as 1676. He certainly was of age at that time. He died in 1741. Will probated 1746, about 65 years after he purchased land in Shrewsbury, N. J., so he must have been about 76 years old when he died.

Caleb Shreve married Sarah Areson, daughter of Deidreck or Derick Areson, born about 1680. He is described as a "Planter" and while his name appears in various ways he called himself "Shrene." He purchased a home at Mt. Pleasant, in Mansfield Township, Burlington county, N. J., that has remained in the possession of the family ever since.

Caleb Shreve died in 1741. His wife, Sarah, was living in 1735. The exact date of her death is not known.

It is not known whether the first Caleb Shreve was a "Friend" or not. He was extremely wealthy and provided handsomely for all of his sons except Benjamin,, before his death.

He lived after 1699 in Burlington county, not far from the present site of Mount Holly, N. J.

Caleb Shreve (2) probably fifth child and fourth son of Caleb Shreve (1) and Sarah Areson, married Mary Atkinson—see will of Thomas Atkinson, New Jersey. (First wife) Caleb Shreve of Burlington county, will dated October 22, 1740, names wife, Ann, sons Amos and Caleb, daughters Rachel and Mary Shreve. See also will of Mary Budd, Northampton Township, Burlington county, dated November 23, 1793, leaves legacies to Beulah, wife of Samuel Brown, also sister's four children, among whom is Kesiah Taylor, wife of Beriah Taylor. Reference: West Jersey Wills, Lib. 33, page 32.

From Atkinson's "History of New Jersey" will of Thomas Atkinson, dated 1739—names fifth child Mary, born 1702, married Caleb Shreve, Jr., 1718—(evidently first wife as will of Caleb Shreve names wife Ann).

(The above data may be found in the Fairmont, W. Va. city library. I have not been able to verify as to whether this line ties up with the local Shreve family. There would be at least one or two generations between the two Benjamins.)

SHREVE GENEALOGY

One Benjamin Shreve married in 1805, Eve Ice. (Monongalia county records.) Jacob Shreve, who came from Kingwood, Wetzel county, to Piggott's Run, married Polly Fortney.

Children of Jacob and Polly (Fortney) Shreve

1, Hannah, married ——— Holderman.
2, Benjamin, married Rachel Willey, of Kingtown, Wetzel county, W. Va.
3, Joshua, married ——— Tichnell.
4, Polly, married Jacob Fortney. (Parents of Nancy Fortney Griffin of Lumberport.)
5, Fielden, married.
6, John, married Jane Gawthrop. (See below.)
7, Nancy, married ——— Griffith, (grandparents of Judge Arlos Harbert).
8, Marion, married.
9, Mary Anne, married William (Little Billy) Martin of Pine Bluff (parents of Jerry, Ulysses E. and L. W. (Otto) Martin.

Children of Benjamin and Rachel (Willey) Shreve

Silas, Ellis, Henry, Augustus, Isaac, Marion, Tabitha, Ruth, and Zilpah. Silas married Jane Taylor, formerly of Waynesburg, Pa. They lived all their married life at Burchfield, Wetzel county, W. Va.

Children of Silas and Jane (Taylor) Shreve.

1, Benjamin, deceased; 2, Rachel Ann; 3, James Reason, farmer, married Edith Cathers; 4, Mary Catharine, married George Sale; 5, Eliza Myrtle; 6, Francis; 7, John Clyde, Ph.D., University of Pittsburgh.

John Clyde married Olive Hixenbaugh, and is a member of the faculty in Glenville State Teachers College. Their children are John Willard and Robert Dayton, Fred and Don.

Francis Shreve, Ph.D. from Peabody College and member of the faculty of Fairmont State Teachers College, married, first, Elma Ruth Cobb who died September 13, 1931. Marriage date June 3, 1920. Their children, Irvin Cobb and Agnes Ellinore.

Francis Shreve married second, Anne Glass on June 16, 1934.

Children of John and Jane (Gawthrop) Shreve.

1, Albert, died with quinsy contracted while on a trip down the river with a raft of timber.

2. Adolphus, married first, Janie Piggott, daughter of Milton Piggot. Second, Allie Miller.

3, A. S. (Bis) married Zanna Wolford, daughter of Adam Wolford.

4, Jacob, married Martha Seese. Daughter Merle married ——— Eichorn of Shinn's Run.

5, U. Grant, married Alice Shreve, daughter of Joshua Shreve. 6, Myrtle died young.

Children of Adolphus and Jane (Pigott) Shreve.

1, Remmie, married Lorna Maulsby; one daughter, Alma. (See Harbert genealogy.)

2, Daisy, married Nathan Harbert. Their children:

Children of Adolphus and Allie (Miller) Shreve: Okey and Harlan.

Children of Grant and Alice (Shreve) Shreve

1, H. M., of Leewood, W. Va; 2, T. L., of Livonia, Pa.; 3, Nina married ——— Janes.

Children of Bis and Zanna (Wolford) Shreve

1, Lester, married Savilla McDaniel; 2, Chester, married Dorothy McDaniel; 3, Beulah, married John Stires, of Lumberport; 4, Martha; 5, Mabel married, Chester Martin, of Worthington.

Children of Nathan and Daisy (Shreve) Harbert
(See Harbert)

1, Jeremiah, married Martha Nay. Children: Jerry, Jr., Nancy Joan, and Fred Wayne; 2, Edward, married Louise Tetric, daughter of L. M. Tetric: One son, Ronald Edward; 3, Margaret, married first, Ray Sander; second, V. E. Lowery.

STURM GENEALOGY.

The Pennsylvania archives show that Johan Jacob Sturm arrived in America from Rotterdam August 21, 1750. See History of Sturm Family, by Margaret H. Sturm.

Jacob (1), Jacob (2), Daniel (3), Asbury Pool Sturm (4).

Asbury P. Sturm, born July 3, 1827, near Worthington, W. Va., married first, August 3, 1848, to Mary Ann Hardesty, born April 4, 1830, daughter of James and Mary (Lane) Hardesty. She died March 1, 1892; he died April 20, 1906. His second wife, Eliza Jane Ridge.

Children of A. P. and Mary A. (Hardesty) Sturm

Minerva Jane, born August 24, 1849; married April 19, 1867, James Snodgrass. Second husband, U. S. Atha.

Laverna C., born October 12, 1853; married May 19, 1872, Jasper Wince; died 1909.

Laura A., born March 28, 1853, married July 17, 1878, J. D. Morgan, (born October, 1856) died May 3, 1924.

Dora, born January 18, 1861; married August 13, 1882, Charles F. Johnson, born 1854.

A. S. Lee, born January 28, 1864; married October 17, 1889, Lora Cochrane.

Byron Ashby, born January 5, 1867; married July 4, 1889, Margaret Moats, born April 18, 1866.

Luella K., born October 18, 1870; married December 9, 1894, William W. Hess, born May 2, 1867, died October 4, 1932.

Jessie M., born December 11, 1874; married January 3, 1897, Melvin Hess, born October 26, 1866, died 1936.

Blanche, born September 20, 1877; married May, 29, 1904, C. D. Willison, born 1874, died 1915.

Daughter of Asbury and Eliza (Ridge) Sturm

Elizabeth Bryan Sturm, born August 14, 1897.

Children of Jane Snodgrass Atha

1, Verna; 2, Georgia; 3, Charles; 4, Lily.

Only child of Jasper and Laverna Wince, Smith Wince.

Children of J. D. and Laura (Sturm) Morgan.

1, Gertrude, married James D. Winger; 2, Lillian, married J. Paul McClintock; 3, Ernest, married Rose Flowers, of Mannington, W. Va.

Children of James D. Winger and Gertrude (Morgan) Winger.

1, Leland H., married Rebecca Slaven. One daughter, Anne Morgan Winger, born April 27, 1938.

2, Robert, born January 1, 1913.

Children of J. Paul and Lillian (Morgan) McClintock

1, Garth, married Maxine Hunter; one daughter, Cherrie, and another baby girl; 2, Robert, married Martha Kelley; one son, Robert, Jr.; one daughter, Patricia.

Children of Ernest and Rose (Flowers) Morgan.

Harold, Charles, Laura, Gertrude, Ernest, Jr., and Billy.

Children of Charles and Dora (Sturm) Johnson

1, Grace, born August 26, 1884, died 1890; 2, Cecil, born 1886, died, 1918; 3, Ossa, born 1891, died 1924; 4, Virginia Evelyn, born September 4, 1901.

Children of Ashby and Margaret (Moats) Sturm

1, H. Glenn, born October 26, 1890, married October 8, 1912, Ethel Reynolds; 2, Mary Effie, born August 3, 1892, married August 23, 1917, Edward R. Shmier; 3, Edna, born October 9, 1894, married July 28, 1929, Raymond Lewis Dennison; 4, G. Edgar, born July 28, 1896, married December 23, 1920, Ruby Willard; 5, William Otto, born January 28, 1899, married July 1, 1920; 6, Darhl H., born May 10, 1900; 7, Maud, born January 16, 1906.

Children of William and Jessie (Sturm) Hess
Mannington,, W. Va.

1, Harold Clare, born November 28, 1897, married December 25, 1924, Fonda Hall; 2, Nell Craven, born Sept. 17, 1900, married Sept. 26, 1925, Louis Watt Cantalou, Albuquerque, N. M.; 3, Lester Clay, born June 28, 1903, attorney; 4, Charles Corbin, born October 4, 1907, teacher.

Children of William and Ella (Sturm) Hess,
Wyatt, W. Va.

1, Raymond Cline, born December 1, 1896, married August 23, 1917, Wanda Ashcraft; 2, Mary Merle, born March 14, 1899; 3, Geneva Ione, born February 7, 1902; 4, Mildred, born June 14, 1905.

THE WAMSLEY FAMILY AT BIG ELM FARM

Although the Wamsleys did not live in this immediate neighborhood, they are the ancestry of a great majority of families herein, as we will discover by studying these family records which I have collected over a period of nearly ~~two~~ 5 years, searching the records in the court houses of Harrison, Marion, and Monongalia counties.

David Wamsley settled on the Big Elm farm as long ago as 1774. He came there about the same time the Robinson's came to Prospect Valley. The will of his father, John Wamsley, Sr., recorded in Augusta county, Virginia, shows that David Wamsley had a sister, Elizabeth, and a brother, John, Jr., who married a brother and a sister of Maj. Benjamin Robinson, namely, McKinney and Mary Robinson respectively.

See on another page where two of David Wamsley's daughters married two of Maj. Benjamin Robinson's sons also.

David Wamsley was a Revolutionary soldier, and is buried on the high hill of the Big Elm farm.

In my mind's eye I can see that large family of girls and boys playing around that giant tree, yes, and in later years those daughters entertaining their beaus; the many romances and love stories the old tree could have told us if it had a voice!

The tree has long since gone, and the log house is fast falling into decay. I have tried to preserve its memory in some paintings and pen and ink drawings. I like to think of the Wamsley family living there, and try to forget the story that has been so impressed on our minds in the book "Daughter of the Elm," which is in no way connected with the Wamsley family. In reading these family records, you can picture for yourself the young men in their Sunday best, going down to Wamsleys to see their best girls. Several Robinsons married into this family. So did two of my own great grandfathers, Wm. Lucas and Robert Bartlett.

_____

_____

_____

_____

DAVID WAMSLEY, SON OF JOHN, SR., AND ──────

Died in Harrison county March, 1849.

Came from Augusta county, Va., to Big Elm farm, Shinnston, W. Va., in 1774. Was a Revolutionary soldier.

His will, recorded in Harrison county Clerk's office, book 6, page 7, dated May 21, 1841, codicil was dated March 27, 1845. Order of probate dated March or August 1849. He married Sarah (Sallie) Delay. Their children:

1. Mary, born January 8, 1782; died January 27, 1852; married Joshua Smith. (Chas. Hornor's line.)

2. Elizabeth, born October 15, 1783; married Jonathan Woods.

3. David B., second, married 1815, Polly Bartlett, daughter of James P. Bartlett.

4. Hannah, born June 20, 1787; married Robert Bartlett (my great grandfather.)

5. Sarah, born June 23, 1790; married 1809, David Robinson (son of Major Benjamin).

6. Absalom, married 1824, Anne Campbell.

7. Rebecca, born September 24, 1795; died May 16, 1875; married John Robinson.

8. Annie, born 1798; died July 9, 1837; married Jacob Smith.

9. Abner G., married Lavina Shinn, daughter of Samuel and Sarah Shinn.

10. Abia P., married Elizabeth Campbell.

11. Tobitha, born September 15, 1803; died August 7, 1872; married September 7, 1830, Samuel Boggess.

Geology of the Valley
By Marshall W. Ogden

The inhabitants of Prospect Valley community today concern themselves somewhat with the known history of its inhabitants since the advent of the white man, and this record has been well developed by the writer of the chapters hereinbefore contained, but from a geological point its history may likewise prove interesting, though derived from the pen of no writer and found only in earth's stratas of stones, shales and sediment.

This unwritten history speaks from the bowels of the earth; not of the achievements of man, or his faults, but of periods and times; not numbered by years but by ages in which the earth was being fitted for the habitation of man and stored with minerals and substances necessary for his comfort.

It is written in the stratas of stone, coal and oil sands, as interpreted by every geologist of authority, that the surface of the earth forming the community of Prospect Valley has a common geological history substantially the same as all of the State of West Virginia, Eastern Ohio and Western Pennsylvania. Here is found the great coal veins, formed by decaying vegetation, stratas of limestone, formed by the shells of deep water animal life, and the oil sands, formed by the combination of decaying sea animal and vegetable products. Each in its turn recording the fact that before the advent of man on the earth this vast expanse of the earth's surface was an inland lake or sea, sometimes deeply covered with water as during the formation of the limestone stratas; at other and different times a marshy lake, as during the formation of the various stratas of coal abounding in this valley.

The depth of this inland lake or sea during the greatest submersion has never been ascertained, as the deepest well ever drilled in this State did not extend through the stratified stone to the bed of this lake or sea. The great system of mountains known as the Alleghenies were formed by a shrinkgae of the surface of the earth causing the land to wrinkle and form mountains, creating the great water shed or drainage system between the Atlantic Ocean and the Ohio and Mississippi valleys.

The bottom of this inland sea or lake was at least three miles below the top of the highest portion of the land. Geologists say that waters of this great inland lake broke through its shores near Salem in Harrison county, where it spread over Eastern Ohio as a marsh and finally emptied into the Great Lakes. That later the vast fields of snow and ice accumulated in the North, gradually melted and as they melted were slowly thrown South by the force of gravitation in the form of glaciers, blocked the outlet of this inland sea on the Northwest and the water was thrown back upon itself, where it eventually found an outlet forming the Ohio and Mississippi rivers. During the various shifts upward and downward of the earth's surface during the untold ages, this inland sea or lake was being filled up by natural causes, such as erosion, the various veins of limestone, coal, gravel, shale, etc., were in turn being formed therein, and by a final upheaval a large portion of this strata was placed well above sea level, where the finger of time, through rains, frosts and freezes, cut great gaps therein and exposed to the surface many of the coal and limestone formations, making them available to man as a commodity. The uses of which have untold possibilities.

The untold ages required to form the various stratas of minerals with which this valley is blessed is perhaps the most interesting from a geological standpoint. Could one stand on the shore of this great inland sea during part of this period, he would behold a dense mass of trees, shrubbery and vines to prodigious heights, foliage so dense the rays of light can scarcely penetrate it, the air is hot and sultry, the waters are rapidly condensed into vapor, forming mist or clouds, through which flap and scream vast numbers of birds and bats of giant size and wing spread, on the low ground and in the shallow water reptiles hiss, mighty mastodons or elephants with curved tusks, wearing coats of long shaggy hair and flowing manes, roam in vast herds, the great cave bear, as large as a horse, fierce and shaggy, stalks his prey, the tiger crouches by the babbling brook and as the wild cattle come down to drink, he leaps on the back of one and feeds from his quivering bleeding body. The air is full of the roar of beasts as they fall upon each other with tooth and claw and gorge themselves on the flesh of their dying prey. The foliage grows rapidly in the damp and humid atmosphere. It matures, falls down, decays and forms nourishment for further masses which grow up in its place, forming a cushion or strata of rotting vegetation of great depth. The waters rise, sediment is cast thereon and as the ages roll on, its carbon becomes coal.

Passing from the unwritten history of this valley as disclosed only by its geological strata in its rocks and mineral stratas to the time is was inhabited by man, we will pause only to say that it is likely the Mound Builders were here, as they were an agricultural race of people, dwelt along the rivers in the valleys and left burial mounds at no great distance in all directions from this region.

Let us stand for a moment on the summit of one of the gently sloping hills surrounding this valley and try to contemplate the untold ages required by nature to create the vast storehouse of fuel, of which this valley is a part. Let us say it in the words of the historian, Ridpath—"so rich in resources, so varied in products, so magnificent in physical aspects. Soil and climate, the distribution of woods and lakes and rivers, the interposition of mountain ranges, and the fertility of valley and forests, here contribute to give man a many sided development.

"Here he finds bays for his shipping, rivers for his steamers, fields for his plow, iron for his forge, gold for his cupidity, landscape for his pencil, sunshine enough for song and snow enough for courage."

The Indians in turn had ceased to dwell in Western Virginia when this valley was first visited by white men. Yet as evidence of their former residence here, they left their arrow heads, flints and mussel shells, strewn about the valley.

Continual and persistent wars among the different tribes made Central West Virginia unsafe for their towns and villages. It was therefore used only as hunting grounds or highway for war parties of Indians passing to and from their forays upon each other. In close proximity to this valley were two well defined buffalo paths or Indian trails passing from the towns and villages of the Massawamees, west of the Ohio River, to the Cherokees, the Chickasaws and Catawbas on the Potomac and James rivers with whom they were continually at war.

One of the trails passed from the Ohio River up Middle Island Creek, over on the waters of Tenmile Creek near the village of Brown, down the creek to its mouth at Lumberport, down the West Fork to the Monongahela and thence to the mouth of White Day Creek. The other passed up Fishing Creek and over on to Buffalo and down by Mannington to the Monongahela by way of Palatine, a camping site; thence to White Day Creek, where it joined the Middle Island trail, then up White Day Creek and over near the neighborhood of Kingwood and over the mountains to the Potomac and James rivers. Neither of these well beaten paths passing directly through this valley, it was spared much of the Indian forays suffered by other parts of Central West Virginia. Only two of these forays resulted in the loss of life to the settlers. One at Harbert's

Fort on Jones Run, and the other the Cunninghams on Cunningham's Run.

We shall now go back to the year 1764, 157 years after the first settlement at Jamestown, when George Washington was 32 years old, 144 years after the landing of the Pilgrims at Plymouth, one year before the passage of the Stamp Act in 1765, the fourth year of the reign of King George III, one year before Patrick Henry made his celebrated speech before the House of Burgesses, one year after France had ceded to England the Dominion of Canada, 12 years before the Declaration of Independence when all of West Virginia was in the District of West Augusta, and any resident therein was a subject of Great Britain.

John Simpson, a trapper and hunter, had his camp at the head of the Youghiogheny River in the glades, at the present location of Moorefield. He employed John and Samuel Pringle, two Englishmen who came to America as soldiers for England in the French and Indian war, deserted at Fort Pitt in 1761, came up the Monongahela River and hid in the forests of Preston county for three years, then went to the head of the Youghiogheny and met John Simpson at Moorefield in Hardy county, and their acquaintance ripened into friendship. The game was getting scarce on account of the many hunters in the glades, so they decided to go further west, and following an old Indian trail called McCulloch's Path and the Horseshoe Trail by way of Gorman, Fairfax Stone and Kingwood, crossing Cheat River at the Horseshoe and came to the Valley River at the mouth of Pleasants Creek about five miles above Grafton. Here he and the Pringles quarreled and separated. The Pringles went up to the mouth of the Buckhannon River and ascended it to Turkey Run, where they hid in a hollow sycamore tree. Here they lived, subsisting on game until 1767 when they ran out of powder and John returned to the South Branch for supplies. He found the French and Indian war ended and no longer in fear of arrest for desertion, returned to his brother, Samuel, who had suffered greatly for want of food, his last charge of powder had long been fired in killing a buffalo, and his only defense from animal or man was his hunting knife. Samuel Pringle then guided South Branch settlers to the Buckhannon River region.

John Simpson, after his quarrel with the Pringles, crossed the Valley River and came to a creek which he named Simpsons Creek and followed it to where it emptied into the West Fork at Clarksburg. Here he established his camp and resided for one year, spending the winter in hunting and trapping beaver, buffalo, deer, and fur bearing animals which he found in abundance. In the summer he whiled away his time in exploring the rivers and valleys, keeping away from the Indian trails, lest his place of abode be revealed to them. There can be no doubt that he, in his meanderings, followed the West Fork River to its junction with the Valley River at Fairmont, and in doing this became the first white man to cast his eyes on the Prospect Valley community.

Let us look at him in our imagination as he stood in solitude on the top of one of the adjacent hills late in April, 1765 and gazed out upon this beautiful valley. He is short of stature, his face is covered with beard, he stands erect, his bearing shows he is yet comparatively a young man and indicates military training. His wearing apparel is a hunting shirt, leggings and moccasins of deerskin, a coonskin cap is on his head, the handle of a hunting knife projects from his belt, a leather pouch and a powder horn are suspended by a strap around his shoulder and his flint lock rifle is in his left hand with the butt resting on the ground. He pays no attention to the dozen or so buffaloes quietly grazing in the valley under the age-old sugar trees, a black she bear with two small cubs pass by him in search of grubs, two deer feeding from the tender shoots of shrubbery on a bench of the hill below him, yet he pays no attention to them, their hides are worthless at this time of the year and as to meat, he has plenty and to spare, his powder and lead are precious and must not be wasted. He makes a mental note of this valley as a desirable place to hunt and trap, then passes on.

Later that year with his store of skins and furs on his back he returned to the settlements on the South Branch, sold his furs, returned to Simpson Creek, built himself a cabin and sold his tomahawk rights to Simpsons Creek in 1772 to John Powers. Simpson formed the acquaintance of Ebenezer Zane and the Robinsons at Moorefield and through this friendship the ancestors of the Robinsons of Prospect Valley were induced to settle here.

Simpson at one time became indebted to one, Cottrill, for one quart of salt and was to pay when he returned from Winchester to sell his furs. He returned without the salt, and they quarreled. Cottrill ran out of the cabin, grabbed Daniel Davisson's gun and attempted to shoot Simpson through the space between the logs. Simpson ran out, wrenched the gun from Cottrill's hands and killed him, which is believed to be the first homicide of a white man in what is now Harrison county.

On July 12, 1774, the Indian Chief Logan, with seven other Indians came upon William Robinson pulling flax with Thomas Hellem and Clayburn Brown in a field opposite the mouth of Simpsons Creek. Brown was shot and Hellem and Robinson ran. Hellem was old, and was soon caught. Robinson was young and would have escaped, but looking back to see if he was gaining, butted into a tree and was knocked senseless. He was captured and carried a prisoner to the Indian camp. He was ordered burned at the stake, but was rescued by Logan, who cut his bonds, took him to a squaw by whom he was adopted, and resided with her until the end of the war when he was exchanged.

www.ingramcontent.com/pod-product-compliance
Lightning Source LLC
Chambersburg PA
CBHW020651300426
44112CB00007B/338